My Studio

Grand Prize, ART USA, 1958
Madison Square Garden, New York

PAINTING AND DRAWING IN

Charcoal

AND **Oil**

EDMOND J. FITZGERALD

REINHOLD PUBLISHING CORPORATION
New York

To Mary Lou

ACKNOWLEDGMENT

The author wishes to thank the following for their kindness

in permitting works of his from their collections to be

reproduced in this book: Mr. Pelham McClellan, Mr. Theodore

Riegel, Miss Minnie Haltin, The Seamen's Church Institute,

The United States Naval War College, and the White Laboratories.

CONTENTS

(Continued on next page)

APPENDIX

List of Color Plates

THE REALM OF CHARCOAL AND OIL

This book embarks upon an adventure in line and color. Its intention is to take the student or amateur artist, through the enchanting realm of pictorial expression in CHARCOAL AND OIL. It is based upon two major themes: first, the interdependence and intimate relationship between drawing and painting; and second, the fundamental character of working directly from nature as the source and fountainhead of art.

No intention is implied to advance an argument against the various bypaths from the great highroad of tradition encountered in many interesting "isms" of contemporary painting, but rather it is maintained that the best equipment for exploring these bypaths, or countless new ones for that matter, is a thorough understanding of the fundamental principles of representational painting.

This excursion is, intentionally, a brief one. It offers but a glimpse of the bright vistas that will be opened. The desire is to stir the interest and adventurous spirit of the reader, and reveal a few guide posts that may point the way to his own personal adventure.

The illustrations are all drawings or paintings of my own. This is to ensure clarity in the step-by-step nature of the demonstrations and in the sequence of the chapters that follow. The fundamental principles that are stressed, and the level of approach, will, it is hoped, fill a need for guidance felt by many students and "Sunday painters." The advanced amateur, and professional, may also find special methods and "shop talk" that will interest him in the pages that follow.

Edmond J. Fitzgerald

LARCHMONT, N. Y.
September, 1958

1

FIRST WE NEED A DRAWING

The great Michelangelo has said "Drawing is painting and painting is drawing." It is my belief that when the profound truth of this statement comes home to the student a great many other things also become clear. Consequently, I have devoted an important part of this book to the subject of drawing.

A drawing can be a terse statement of a few lines, or a fully rendered tonal study. It can be done with the finest point (i.e. an etching needle), a blunt block of crayon or a brush already charged with color. It may exist as a complete work in itself, but it is *always* the essential plan of every painting. It is born of the will to express, and is the underlying structure, the very "bones" of the painting. Above all, it does not end when you put down the charcoal and take up the brush, but continues to the final touch of color.

Tools

Drawing tools are many and varied. They include a great many pencils and crayons of varying degrees of hardness and texture. The voluptuous, velvety grain of the lithographers' crayon and the incisive hard graphite of the mechanical draftsman are part of the equipment of drawing. Various colored pencils, crayons and chalks (pastels) can also be considered as part of the draftsman's kit. Observe how easily the transition from black and white to color seems when we are talking of graphic implements.

Drawing tools also include instruments such as "T" squares, triangles, and all those beautiful precision instruments such as dividers, compasses, and so forth, that are used by the architect.

For a discussion of drawing in its fundamental aspects we need only to consider the most primitive but most eloquent of all drawing tools, vine charcoal. Charcoal can be easily sharpened with a piece of sandpaper or other rough surface, and can be erased with a piece of cloth, chamois or kneaded eraser. It works best on a slightly rough surface. Charcoal paper is available in several grades, but almost any paper will do. It is ideally suited to drawing on a primed canvas or panel in preparation for oil painting. Though flexible, charcoal is not well-suited to very small drawing. The

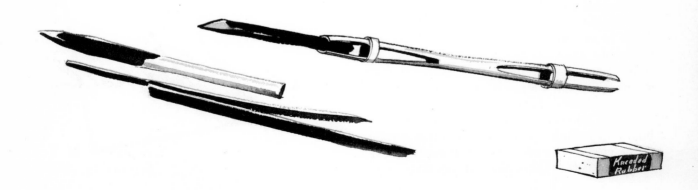

standard size, 19 x 25 inch charcoal paper is ideal for practice drawings.

A board on which to tack the paper, plus a couple of items I will mention directly, and we have all the equipment needed to produce a masterpiece. The items referred to are, first, a measuring stick (the twelve inch handle of an oil painting bristle brush works fine). The second item is a view-finder — a sort of window through which you can observe a subject — thus relating it to a rectangular shape, proportional to the surface on which you plan to draw.

A view-finder can be made by cutting out two "L" shaped pieces of cardboard. These can be formed into a "window" by means of two paper clips. The opening can be adjusted to the proportion of the sheet on which you work, by simply making sure that the diagonals of both coincide (see illustrations).

In observing a subject through the view-finder, the scale can be changed by merely moving the view-finder nearer or further from your eye. Also, of course, the opening can be varied in size. Care must always be exercised to make sure that the opening is in proportion to the outside dimensions of the drawing you are making.

The view-finder is not intended as a window through which to "copy" a subject, but rather as a means to help you focus your attention and decide what you wish to include or exclude from your picture. It will also help you to decide whether your picture shall be upright or horizontal, and where, in relation to its margins, you should locate the major feature or features of the subject.

It will be readily apparent that the cardboard view-finder performs a function similar to the view-finder on a camera. Essential planning of a picture takes place at this stage, and,

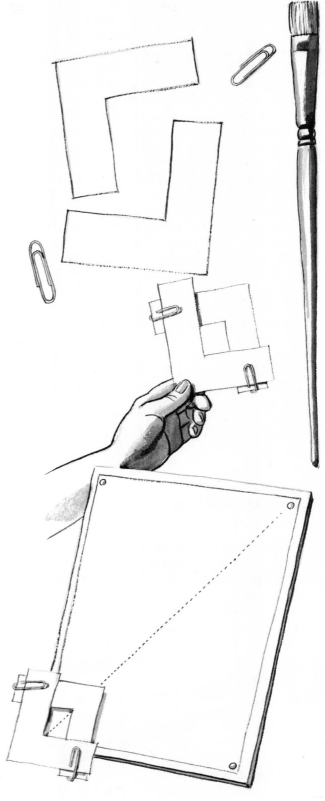

in its most fundamental and elementary aspects, the realm of picture "composition" has been entered.

Consider the problem of transposing something observed to the paper before you. It doesn't make much difference *what* you draw. One fact only is certain — there is no such thing as an "easy" subject. To search for one leads only to heartbreaking disappointment. On the other hand, the beginner who tackles a subject that seems appallingly complex is often surprisingly rewarded for his effort. Contrary to common belief, it is no *easier* to make an accurate drawing of an extended form than of a foreshortened one. If anything, the reverse is true, simply because errors are more readily apparent in the foreshortened form. Similarly, the profile is not easier (also contrary to much preconception) than some other view of the head. In fact, the beginner generally fails more in the construction of a head seen in profile than front view. This is because he is seduced into the belief that a likeness can be obtained by outlining the features alone, and he overlooks the underlying forms indispensible to likeness. Incidently, the usual fault is to make the face too long from brow to chin. In summary, any object or group of objects that remains reasonably still is suitable material for the study of the fundamentals of drawing.

Composition

The word "composition" embraces the ultimate goal of pictorial expression. It is at least one common ground on which all the "isms" of painting meet. I will mention it only briefly here as it will crop up again from time to time in succeeding chapters. It is like certain medicines, in too large a dose it does more harm than good. A few rules, in the form of "don'ts" are helpful in seeking subjects:

Don't divide your picture into too equal parts.

Don't place the most important feature of your subject in the center of the picture.

Don't permit long, straight, or otherwise strong lines to go to the corners of the picture.

Don't hestitate to leave out or shift some feature of your subject if you feel it will improve the picture.

Enough "don'ts" for now. The insidious thing about such rules is that most of them have been successfully broken in masterpieces. The marvel of 20th Century painting is its emancipation. It has shaken off rigid rules — anything goes! Great freedom breeds its own sobering responsibilities, though.

Proportion and Scale

For a demonstration of a way to establish proportion and scale, let us consider the human figure. For the beginner who feels that this subject may be too difficult, let me repeat — it is no harder to draw the figure than anything else (providing the model stays reason-

ably still). One might let more errors go unobserved in drawing, say, a bowl of flowers. That does not mean that the drawing is more correct, however. In the process of learning, a most vital factor is to recognize errors. But to get on with the work, a friend or member of the family seated nearby, with a wall for background, will do. (I find that small sums of money are most persuasive with my children.)

Observe the subject through the view-finder. By adjusting the size of the opening and by moving the view-finder a bit we can decide (1) how much of the figure we wish to include, (2) whether it seems to "compose" best as an upright or a horizontal, (3) where we should place our subject within the frame of the rectangle, and (4) scale: i.e. how large or small the subject appears with reference to the rectangle.

Assume that we have decided to include all of the figure and chair. The head is to be a short distance from the top margin, and the feet very close to the bottom. We make a small mark with the charcoal at these two locations. We have now set a task for ourselves—to make the figure fit within these marks. Now we must determine the proportions. For this we make use of the measuring stick (the brush handle).

The stick is used to make measurements by sighting, using the thumb to indicate the length of the measurement (see illustration). Three things are important to remember in this operation: (1) always keep the arm straight, *no bend at the elbow;* (2) close one eye, (3) the measurements taken are *relative* measurements, to be used to compare one proportion with another, and are *not* to be conveyed directly to the drawing as this would generally result in too small a scale.

By sighting, and comparing, we can determine certain salient facts about the subject. For example, are the hands in the lap about

halfway between the top of the head and the feet? Measure from the top of the head to the hands, and without moving the thumb, shift the sighting arm downward and compare the distance between the hands and feet. If the hands are at the halfway point we can now make a small mark on our drawing halfway between the two already made. We have now begun to establish proportions. The process can be continued to "pin down" a few more points before we really start to draw. For instance, the width of the figure and chair combination appears to be about one-half the height. Using the stick-and-sight method we can soon make sure, and we can put down a few additional points on the drawing. The head makes a good unit of measure. How many "heads" from the top of the head to the hands? By sight measure we determine that there are three. Another mark can go on the paper, one-third of the way between the "head" and "hands" positions already established (see illustration).

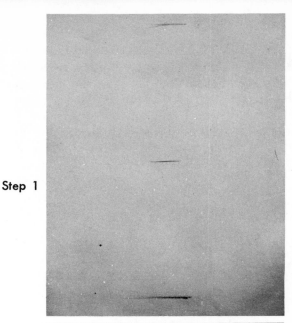

Step 1

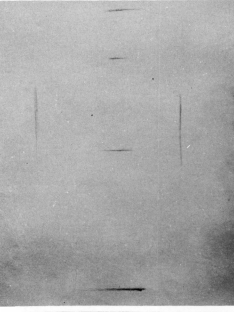

Step 2

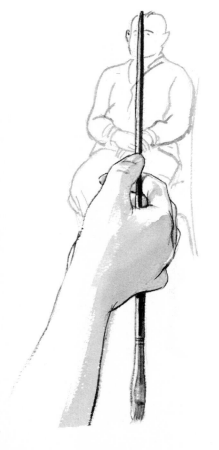

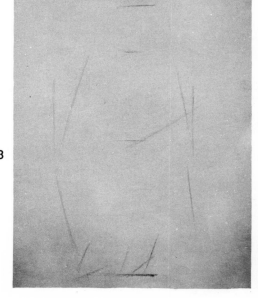

Step 3

Blocking In

It is well to start translating some of the points into shapes before we get too many. However, we will still avoid the precise outline, as premature reference to it can lead us astray from the job at hand which is to establish proportions. We "block in" by drawing very light lines that reduce the shape we observe to its simplest terms. Reduce subtle curving lines to straight ones, but be sure to get the *direction* of the line as true as possible. Also the *distance* the line travels must be carefully observed. Let *direction* and *distance* be watchwords in these blocking in lines. Also

concentrate on the volumes and spaces enclosed by these lines. Don't forget to keep using the sight-measuring stick to check the relative sizes of the shapes as they begin to form on the paper.

Another good use for the stick is in judging vertical and horizontal relationships. For example, hold the stick in a vertical position between your eye and the subject. By sighting past it you can get a fair estimate of the vertical relationships in the subject. Is the hand just under the face? Is the knee just in line with the shoulder? The same system can be used horizontally.

As the blocking in continues, a semblance of the subject begins to emerge.

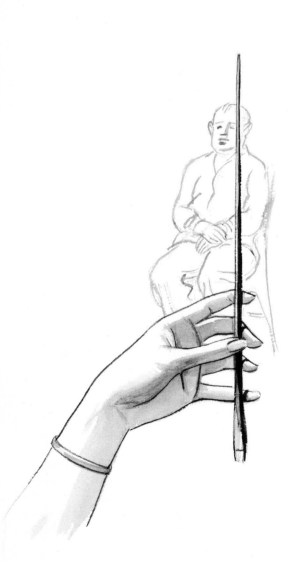

Step 4

Step 5

15

Step 6

Step 7

Contours

As the blocking in assumes more and more the illusion of the subject, the curved lines can be faired in. Do not fall into the evil habit of erasing every line that doesn't seem just right to you. If you feel hesitant and doubtful, draw the line lightly. Several restatements of the line may be necessary. As you gain confidence (and you must try to bolster up your courage) and "find" the true swing of the line, draw it more firmly. The unerased exploratory lines will not matter. They are present in many of the drawings of the great masters: Raphael, Rembrandt, Gericault, Ingres (a noted drawing by the latter for his painting "The Harem" has a complete third arm).

Don't let the outline dominate you; it is tyrannical and will try. Think of it as the passage between the visible and hidden part of the form you draw. Think of the nature of the substance you are drawing, how it would feel to the touch. Remember that one's knowledge of the texture of things comes as much from the sense of touch as sight. An infant in a crib learns to distinguish the difference between substances by touch first, and thus informs his sense of sight. The drawings of a sculptor generally indicate this characteristic more incisively than those of a painter. The painter is more concerned with those elements more implicit to the sense of sight — tone values. The rounding off of forms gives our drawing more life, rhythm, and grace.

Tone Values

Up to this point all our discussion has been about lines, those distances between points so indispensible to the draftsman. They are products of the imagination and intellect. Strictly speaking, there are no "lines" in nature. Lines merely locate the place where the visible and the invisible parts of a form meet. Or the place where one tone meets another. This leads us into the realm of "tone values," or more commonly, "values" — the degree of darkness or light of any area.

Values can be put into our drawings with the same tool we use for lines. But just as lines are indispensible to the draftsman, values are necessary to the painter. The moment you apply a color to any surface you also apply a value. A fundamental, perhaps the *most* fundamental characteristic of any color is its *value* — the amount of darkness or light it possesses.

Learning to judge the relative values in a subject is not easy. It requires real concentration and much practice. It requires especially, seeing with the "painter's eye." That is, seeing things in nature in terms of painting. Half closing the eyes, or squinting, so the vision is dimmed and simplified, helps. Another way is to try looking at a subject without focusing on any one spot—seeing the *whole* at once, more or less equally, but nothing sharply. People who are nearsighted have a certain advantage in this for they have only to remove their glasses to see the world in simplified, out of focus, relationships. Some say that nearsightedness was actually a contributing factor to the so-called impressionism of Monet and Degas.

As you try to draw values in your sketches, do not be too concerned with technique. In putting in values the aim should be to get them down as directly as possible. In time, technical ease will develop of itself. Only in that way is valid technique and "style" developed.

The way a subject is lighted is of paramount importance when we draw the values. Simple lighting from one source is usually best. Keep the shadows broad and simple, but model the light areas as much as you can.

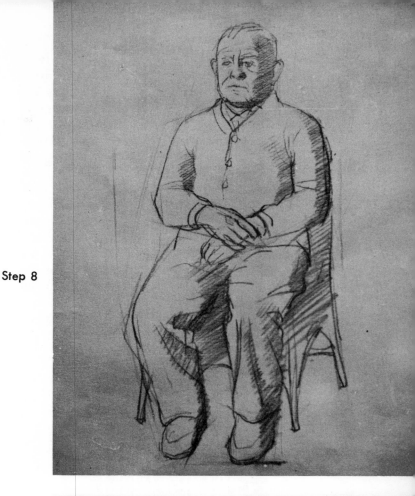

Step 8

Step 9

The bristle brush now comes in handy to smooth out the charcoal tones a bit. Twisted paper "stumps" are also useful for this. Too much smoothing will rob your drawing of freshness, however. Don't overdo it. The kneaded eraser can be pinched into a knife-edge, or point, for the purpose of picking out high lights.

I like to consider values in four main divisions: (1) the high lights; (2) the broad lights; (3) the broad shadows; and (4) the accents — small dark touches. The broad lights and broad shadows (also called middle values) are the largest in area and convey most of the modelling. They also carry most of the color — when we come to that. They should be done first. The accents and high lights are the finishing touches and should be done last.

The dominance of middle values can be demonstrated by drawing on gray or other neutral-toned paper using charcoal or pencil for the darker tones and chalk for the lights.

Thermal Quality

An understanding of values paves the way for the use of color. Aside from value, the chief characteristic of every color is its "thermal" quality, the degree of warmth or coolness it contains. The play of light and shadow—values —over forms reveals the forms to us in a mighty symphony of counterplay between these two opposed forces. In like manner, and intermingling in the magic of this orchestration, is the play and counterplay of warmth and coolness.

Generally speaking, lights are warmer and shadows are cooler, but there are warm depths in the shadows and cool passages shoot through the lights. Also, broadly speaking, warm colors are those that partake of reds and yellows, and cool colors are those that tend toward blue.

By adding a warm color to the charcoal we immediately enter the thermal realm. Sanguine (red) Conté crayon makes a happy marriage with vine charcoal or the more intense artificial charcoal (also called Russian or Siberian charcoal). Observe how the blacks and grays now look cool when opposed by the red. Also note the great variety that can be obtained where the two intermingle. This is the foundation of color.

Figure Study

Sanguine Conté crayon and Russian charcoal were used to express the contrasting warmth and coolness of flesh tones in this study.

19

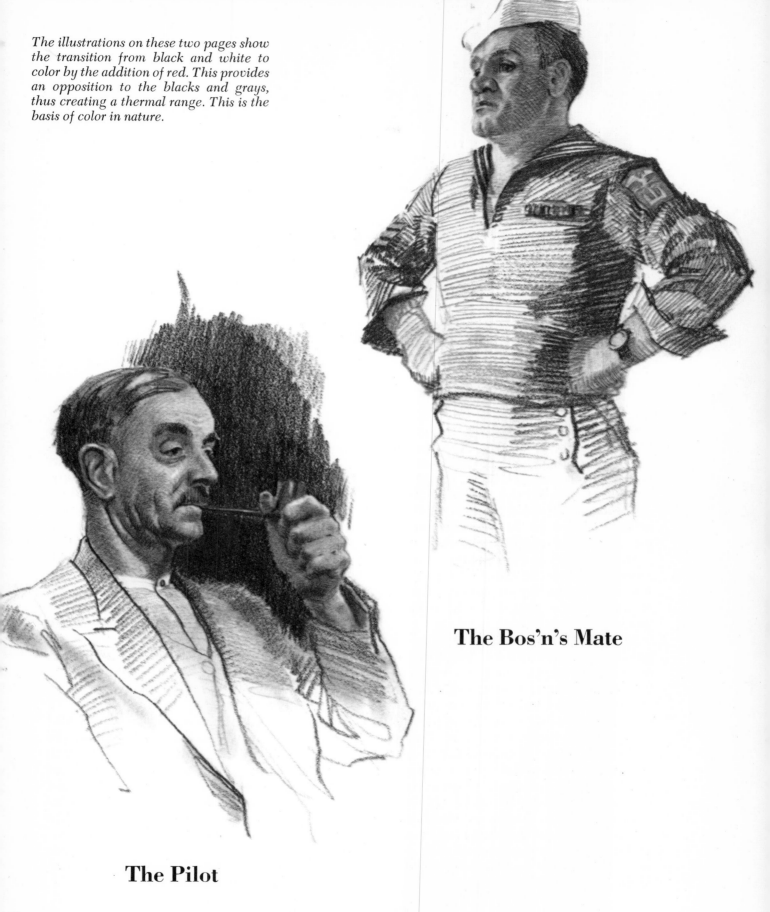

The illustrations on these two pages show the transition from black and white to color by the addition of red. This provides an opposition to the blacks and grays, thus creating a thermal range. This is the basis of color in nature.

The Bos'n's Mate

The Pilot

2

LET'S TRY A FEW OIL COLORS

When asked for a definition of painting, Max Beerbohm said, "It is the spreading of colors on something with the hair of an animal fastened to the end of a stick." It is my intention, also, to simplify this vast subject to workable proportions — not the neat succinctness of Beerbohm — but fundamental enough to provide a useful foundation on which to build.

Many details concerning materials and definitions have been relegated to Appendix A or B to avoid undue interruption of a discussion of "how it's done", and of some historical background.

There is nothing to show that the art of painting improves with the passing of time, or in any sense in pace with man's gain in the field of technology, science, and so forth. The oldest drawings known, from the caves of Lascaux and Altamira, evoke feelings of understanding and response from us. They want nothing in the way of improvement or an added gadget — unlike last year's automobile. Nevertheless, artists have adopted for their use, from the passing parade of technological change, some few innovations that have augmented the ease of their labors and the transportability and permanence of their productions. Perhaps the most noteworthy example of this concession to the progress of the Great

World was the development during the Renaissance of the technique of oil painting.

The brothers Van Eyck, in northern Europe, and Antonella da Messina and Bellini, in Italy, produced some of the earliest oil paintings that have come down to us. Some scholars proclaim that the technique is much older and it seems reasonable to assume that earlier artists would have tried mixing their pigments with various resins and oils — to make them stick — as well as with egg yolk or some other adhesive material. The important thing to us is that the method is a long established, convenient way of "drawing" in color.

Art materials of today are quite different from those of the Renaissance. They are highly standardized and readily obtainable — even in small towns.

Art training is also readily available. Museums and art schools flourish throughout the land and even where they are not plentiful, books and fine prints are. All may take heart from the fact that some of the world's most renowned painters were self-taught. These include not only the so-called "primitives" like Edward Hicks or Grandma Moses, but some of the most sophisticated masters: Jean Louis Meissonier, Sir Thomas Laurence, and Gustave Courbet — to name a few.

Elementary Outfit

The basic equipment for oil painting consists of:

Paints — tube colors
Brushes — at least 4
Support — canvas or panel, etc.
Mediums — turpentine, oil, etc.
Palette — mixing surface
Palette knives
Palette cups — at least 2
Box to carry equipment
Easel

The pigments from which artist's colors are made come from many sources and are often quite different from each other in their physical and chemical properties. Some are simply "earths" taken almost in their natural state. Others are products of elaborate laboratory and industrial processing.

The names of colors are confusing. Some are named for their place of origin, some for the person who discovered or developed them. There are many hues and shades available to the artist today, probably far more than necessary. A few are a great deal more expensive per tube than the average, but, by and large, artists' materials of the best quality are not expensive. One has only to consider that it is — at least theoretically — possible to produce an article of great value for a few dollars in materials. Andrew Mellon paid $747,500 for a 9″ x 12″ by Raphael, St. George and the Dragon (National Gallery of Art, Washington).

Before the industrial revolution the number of pigments available was limited by today's standards, yet some pretty good paintings were somehow produced. It can be easily deduced from this that factors other than the number of available colors governed. One limiting factor that applied then, as now — aside from the incidence of talent — was the limited range of *values* available to the artist. Consider for a moment that black and white pigments mark the limits of the range with which to represent light — from the noonday sun to the shadows in a coal mine.

With the riot of new colors born of the industrial revolution and soon to burst forth in the blaze of impressionism, painters tried to overcome the limits imposed by values and "construct by means of color alone." Along with this came the misguided effort by some to apply to painting the principals of those physical properties of color inherent in light, as revealed by studies of the spectrum. The difficulty here was that colored pigments are vastly different from colored light, and any attempt to make a literal reconciliation of the two was doomed to failure. Suffice it to say that when we add to the black and white range limit of values the thermal quality discussed in Chapter I — and available in a few pigments ranging from warm to cool — we have the basic tools of the old masters available to us.

Oil colors are made by grinding the dry pigments (the same, with a few exceptions, that are used for watercolor, tempera or pastels) into a paste with a liquid vehicle. Linseed oil, of various kinds, forms the basic vehicle or binding material used. Other drying oils and stabilizers are also used for the sake of more or less uniform drying and working qualities of the various pigments. We have merely to apply these colors to a surface to produce a picture.

Canvas, primed with white paint, is the usual surface used, but other surfaces are also suitable. Canvas is preferred because of its lightness and strength and the ease with which large or small sizes can be stretched.

Nearly any smooth nonabsorbent surface will do as a mixing surface or palette. The tear-off type paper palette is quite satisfactory and practical.

A minimum of four brushes will start a beginner painting. A flat sable ¼ inch, or smaller, and three flat bristles, ¼, ½ and ¾ inch, make a practical selection. There are many sizes and types of brushes and painting knives available (see Appendix A). My recommendation is that these be added with some restraint to the beginner's outfit. The reason for this applies with equal force to the addition of various colors, mediums, and other equipment. Painting is such a *personal* experience that close acquaintance with a few items, and the addition of new ones in response to a real need, is more rewarding and ensures a better understanding than taking on too much at once.

As for mediums, turpentine is needed to clean the brushes, and for thin underpainting;

and linseed oil — to be used sparingly — to thin colors as necessary. The subject of mediums has intrigued artists since earliest times. Various materials and mixtures have been tried in the hope of imparting some improvement to the working qualities of paint or the appearance of the painting. The possibilities have by no means been exhausted and you, too, can have fun experimenting. Someone has said, "you can paint with anything that sticks." Obviously the requirement of permanence imposes limitations. There is more information on mediums in later chapters and several good handbooks of materials are listed in the Bibliography.

At least one palette knife is necessary for mixing and general purposes. The knife also makes a good implement for applying paint. Many shapes and kinds are available.

Palette cups for holding mediums should be wide enough to get a one-inch brush into readily. I prefer separate cups rather than those joined together in pairs as it is easier to empty or clean one at a time.

Paint boxes are of metal or wood, and some have folding easels attached. The most popular size is 12 x 16 inches by about 3 inches deep. I use a metal-lined wood one and use a folding aluminum easel for outdoor sketching.

Rags are also necessary. It's a good idea to tear them into small pieces, the size of a handkerchief, so that a clean one is always ready at hand for wiping brushes. Dirty paint rags are combustible and should be discarded after the day's use. They should *never* be kept in an enclosed space.

At the end of a day's painting always wash brushes with soap and tepid water, never hot, as it melts the glue in the ferrule. Rub up a lather in the palm of your hand and work it into the brush, rinsing frequently. Shape the hairs with your fingers, and it is best to dry your brushes hanging or resting with the hairs downward. This helps keep their shape and prevents water from working back into the ferrule.

The Limited Palette

If we substitute black oil paint (Ivory Black) for the black drawing instrument of Chapter I, add white oil paint to give us the other end of the value range, a bright red (Cadmium Red Light or Vermilion) and an "in-between" color (Yellow Ochre), we have a basic palette with remarkable potentials. Add to this the fast-drying, neutral-toned Raw Umber for the lay-in, or underpainting. The virtue of the limited palette is that it avoids the complexity of many hues and keeps us "on the beam" regarding *value* and *thermal* fundamentals.

Posing a Model

For a demonstration of the use of the limited palette let us pose a live model again — as in Chapter I — this time a nude. We'll pose the model against a simple background, with the light falling from one direction only. Four to six poses of twenty five minutes each, with a five minute rest for the model, should suffice for a small study.

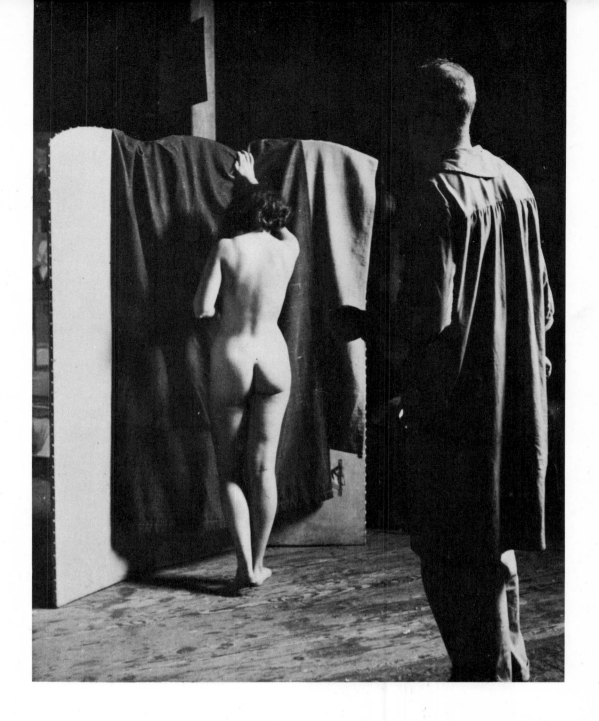

Posing a model is part of the problem of composition. Arranging a still life has a similar relationship to picture making. That is, part of the composing can be done before you start to draw. (Landscape differs in this regard.) Think of the background, lighting, and the pose itself in terms of the finished picture enclosed in a frame (here again the view finder can be helpful). Do not forget the comfort of the model. An overdifficult pose is a hardship to model and artist alike.

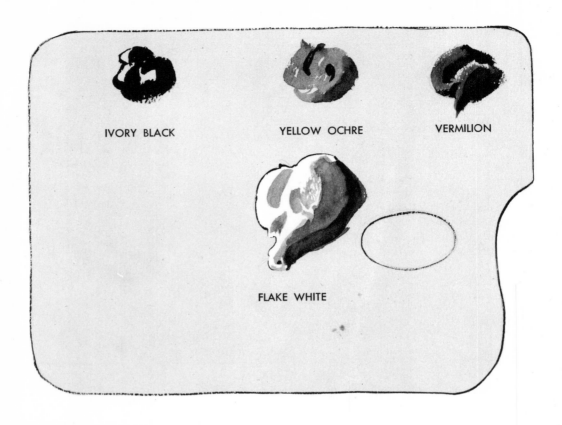

IVORY BLACK   YELLOW OCHRE   VERMILION

FLAKE WHITE

Drawing and Lay-In

The drawing can be done on a 9 x 12 inch canvas with charcoal. The first pose should be devoted to the drawing. Even a greater proportion of time can be devoted to the drawing if necessary. So much depends on the drawing — this cannot be overstressed.

Next, some Raw Umber is squeezed onto the palette and a lay-in of the values is done with a wash of Raw Umber thinned with turpentine. No white is used with this as it would slow the drying. Lighter shades are made by adding turpentine. The purpose of this lay-in is to establish the pattern of the values. When it is done the Umber can be removed from the palette. The lay-in dries quickly and absorbs

most of the charcoal dust; any remaining should be dusted off. About the same length of time should be used for this as for the drawing. In the next stage the lay-in will be practically all covered with heavier paint.

It should be noted here that a consistent method of setting up the palette is desirable. Any systematic arrangement of the colors is acceptable. My own method is to place the colors along the upper margin of the palette commencing on the right with the warmest colors and advancing to the cooler colors on the left. Far more white is used than any other pigment, so it may be isolated from the others and placed nearer the center of the palette.

Step 1

The drawing is done as described in Chapter I. Check the relative proportions by sighting and measuring. Establish the direction and distance each major line takes, and then "fair in" the curves. Carefully locate the shapes of the shadows. A few light shadings will help separate light and shadow patterns.

Step 2

With a medium sized brush (No. 4 flat, on this size canvas) and a neutral color well thinned with turpentine (Raw Umber is my favorite for this) wash in the shapes of the shadows and other large middle values. No white is used, and the thin wash dries quickly — like water color.

Broad Shadows and Broad Lights (Middle Values)

Next a generous portion of White, Yellow Ochre, Ivory Black, and Cadmium Red are squeezed onto the palette and the value of a major shadow area is mixed on the palette. Yellow Ochre and Ivory Black form the basis for this, although both White and Red may be added to achieve the thermal, as well as the value. The paint is applied fairly thin in the dark passages. The broad lights are now mixed on the palette, using Yellow Ochre, Cadmium Red, and White as the basis. A little of the black is added to supply the coolness as needed. The paint is applied more heavily in the light areas.

Step 3

Step 4

Step 5

Accents and Highlights

High lights and accents are put in last. The high lights are put in with a heavy impasto and the accents (small dark touches) are more thinly painted. The high lights are almost pure white and are scooped onto the end of the brush or knife and touched into place deftly so that the paint remains thick enough to catch and flash back the light.

The application of paint should be as *direct* as possible; the fewer the manipulations and scrubbings the better. If a group of strokes do not "go" well, scrape them off with the palette knife and try again. The same principle applies to brush strokes as to "shading" in drawing (page 17). They should not be an end in themselves but a result. One admires the sure, clean, brush work in any masterpiece. It is the "handwriting" of the artist. The brush strokes reveal the most intimate stirrings of inspiration. They augment and reaffirm the universal principle found in all nature and expressed by Leonardo da Vinci in the words "The result flows out of the cause by the shortest possible course." Seek *directness* but not vain cleverness or virtuosity. Even a certain "clumsiness" is preferable when it reveals the sincerity and high endeavor of the artist. This quality also is present in masterpieces: in Cezanne, Eakins, Daumier — even Goya and Rembrandt.

Nude

Limited palette

Ivory Black, Flake White, Yellow Ochre and Cadmium Red are the only colors used in the figure study opposite. As explained in the text, this limited palette serves adequately the fundamental functions of color — value range and thermal range. Reference here is to the representational use of color as opposed to the decorative use. In the latter case (as well as in certain representational problems) more colors are needed. We will go into this in the next chapter.

The two illustrations here are of small paintings done with a limited palette to demonstrate the possibilities for extremely varied subjects that can be done with three or four colors.

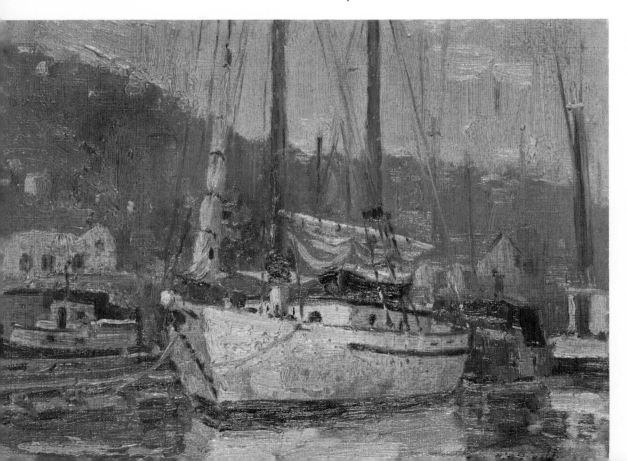

Desme

On the next page is a larger painting (30 x 40) with more involved subject matter done in the same limited palette as the nude demonstrated in this chapter except that a small amount of Viridian Green was added.

3

MORE COLORS AS WE NEED THEM

Adding to the Palette

In the foregoing chapter we discussed a limited palette: Black, Yellow Ochre, Vermilion, and White. It will be noted that blue is conspicuously absent from this palette. The curious fact is that the addition of blue to this group is the proverbial "monkey wrench in the works." The mixture of black and white makes a cool grey, and when used in conjunction with the other two colors only, looks almost blue, and provides the necessary cool element of the thermal range. The addition of blue throws this delicate balance out of adjustment.

Certain colors can be added to the group successfully, however, and still retain it's effectiveness. Viridian, (a strong green) can be used with the group, either as a spot of local color, such as a costume note, or in mixtures.

A good way to test the magic of this limited palette is to use it in making copies of certain old masters. Paintings by such diverse masters as Frans Hals, Velasquez, Goya, and Rembrandt can be successfully copied using only White, Black, Yellow Ochre, and Vermilion.

This palette can be used for certain landscape effects, such as stormy light, or the kind of serene effects in certain Corot's, where there is little blue light. With the sun out, and a bright sky, it fails. There is then a crying need

for blue. Blue in turn calls for something stronger in the yellow range to oppose it, and the palette must be expanded.

There is nothing "wrong" about a more extensive palette. As stated earlier though, intimate acquaintance with a few items provides a strong base on which to expand. There are, of course, other limited palettes. One could invent many combinations that would work, based on the twin needs of (1) range of values, and (2) thermal range — warm and cool — to dovetail into the value range.

One such limited palette I have found effective for outdoor work is: White, Indian Red, Cadmium Yellow, Ultramarine Blue, and Viridian. The yellow, blue, and green (Viridian) provide a considerable green range in combination, and with white added. The red and blue give a wide range of purplish tints and grays in combination with white. The gray range can be extended greatly with small additions of yellow or green. The red, blue, and green together make a strong dark that is almost black in value intensity.

The key to representing nature is not so much in "matching" colors, but in creating the *illusion* of nature, first in the value range, and secondly in the thermal. The use of limited palettes and study of the great masters will help the student to understand this, and will establish a firm base from which to explore further.

A Universal Palette

Paint manufacturers offer many alluring tints and shades with which to expand our palette. The student is strongly advised to sample and relish them, not hastily, but with due consideration — like a gourmet.

The question of permanence should be carefully considered. Buying the best brands is not *ipso facto* assurance of the permanence of all colors, and reliable color makers hasten to explain this in their literature. There are also several thorough and disinterested artists handbooks that give complete information on all pigments (see the Bibliography).

One should only adopt colors with a good reputation for permanence because once you have acquired the habit of using a given color, it is like the tobacco habit — hard to shake. Many artists of high renown use certain colors of doubtful permanence because they simply "can not get along without them."

The insidious thing is that some fugitive colors are of great beauty. Also, certain colors have great permanence under some conditions and are very fugitive under others. Emerald Green, for example, is permanent by itself, but will turn black when mixed with the cadmiums and some other colors. Emerald Green has, incidentally, the additional hazard of being extremely poisonous. White Lead, Cobalt Violet, and Malachite Green are also poisonous.

There are a few colors of borderline permanence that many artists find indispensable for special problems, such as flower painting or to represent certain fabrics. Alizarin Crimson is such a color, Prussian Blue another. Hooker's Green, a very popular water color, is a mixture of Prussian Blue and Gamboge, (both fugitive).

The varied aspects of this problem are too complex to be covered in the scope of this book. It provides an interesting field for one to explore.

Each individual should arrive at his own choice of colors ultimately anyway, as this is the most personal part of the art of painting. It is, therefore, more reasonable to start with a few and add rather cautiously, than to start with too many.

My own palette, arrived at over the years, contains, in addition to White, 13 colors, as follows:

Alizarin Crimson	Burnt Sienna
Indian Red	Raw Umber
Cadmium Red Light	Viridian
Cadmium Orange	Cobalt Blue
Cadmium Yellow	Ultramarine Blue
Cadmium Yellow Pale	Ivory Black
Yellow Ochre	

I find this palette universal enough for most subjects. Sometimes I use an additional color or two for some special purpose, however as stated earlier, I often confine my work to a much more limited palette.

White is a key pigment and merits special consideration. Far more of it is used in oil painting than any other pigment. White Lead, usually called Flake White, or Cremnitz White, is the white of the old masters. It has superlative working qualities and hiding power. It has a tendency to yellow somewhat with age, or if exposed to sulphur-bearing fumes, hence since about 1850 it has been supplanted on many artists' palettes by Zinc or (since 1920) Titanium Whites, or by mixtures of the two. Some of the vices of White Lead have been eliminated by this substitution, but its excellent qualities have not been equalled. Perhaps the concern about the tendency of White Lead to yellow slightly is in the nature of "choking at a gnat and swallowing a camel," in view of the yellowing tendencies of the oils used in paint and other hazards involved. It is still the white of the Old Masters!

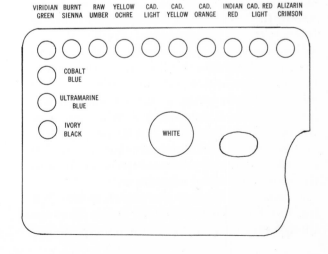

Mediums

Many experiments, speculations, and several books have been inspired by the subject of painting mediums. Some of the books are listed in the Bibliography.

The function of a painting medium is to assist in the application, working qualities, and final appearance of paint. The principal substance involved in painting mediums is usually one of the drying oils: linseed oil (in various forms), poppy oil, walnut oil, Perilla oil, tung oil, lumbang oil, and so forth. Various resins (natural and synthetic), beeswax, alumina hydrate, zinc stearates and other substances are used to impart gloss, a buttery consistency, or some other desired quality. When one considers that each pigment has its own idiosyncrasies, it becomes apparent that a vast and complex system of relationships is involved in the search for ideal admixtures.

It may well be that the search is like that for the fabled Fountain of Youth. Perhaps there is no such thing as an ideal medium, but the search is alluring, and the mysterious appeal of ancient recipes will always have devotees. The enthusiasm of the hunt may lend vigor to the resultant pictures, and with good fortune, disaster may not be an accompanying handmaiden.

It is said that certain 19th Century painters thought they had discovered, in the use of bitumen, the secret of Rembrandt. This warm and luminous substance (which never dries) brought ruinous results when used excessively. At least one painter, Munkácsy, was led to insanity by the spectacle of much of his life's work deteriorating before his eyes, because of this material.

The combined effect of mineral spirit mixed with colors and used on an absorbent ground to achieve a mat effect, has also produced some fragile paintings. One Degas is kept under glass at the Metropolitan Museum because the surface tends to dust off like pastel, probably as a result of such an experiment.

Setting up a flower subject is similar to posing a model in that many of the problems of composition can be solved at this stage. In the drawing and painting one can certainly alter the forms and colors of nature to improve the picture, but all consideration should be given to arrange the best set-up possible. The color masses of the flowers, the lighting, the vase, and the background should all reflect the artists feelings of a paintable subject.

A Flower Piece

For a demonstration of the use of an augmented palette, let us consider a flower piece. We will surely need a wider range of colors than the limited palette discussed in Chapter II, so I shall lay out the group of 14 colors listed earlier in this chapter.

The method of approach in painting flowers is also dictated somewhat by the perishable nature of the subject. That is, it must be fairly fast.

To achieve speed, I shall use a smooth panel of masonite instead of canvas. Two coats of thinned white paint have been previously applied to the masonite as a painting ground. The hard surface offers little "drag" to the brush and a minimum of absorbency to the paint, thus enabling faster work.

Alla Prima

A very direct, or *alla prima,* method of painting will also be the speediest, and is in harmony with the subject and the working surface selected.

Giving due consideration to the placement of flowers, vase, and a couple of pieces of drapery to make a harmonious ensemble, I will study the subject a bit through the view-finder and then set to work with charcoal directly on the white surface. The size of the panel is 20 x 24 inches.

When I feel that a satisfactory, rough layout has been accomplished, I switch to pencil and go over the charcoal lines. I do this to refine the drawing, and also to permit the dusting off of the charcoal before applying paint. To speed up the process I plan to eliminate the intermediate step of monotone lay-in used on the figure painting in Chapter II.

When the drawing is completed, in about one-quarter of a four to six hour period allowed for the painting, I plunge in like a boy in the old swimmin' hole. With a one-inch brush, fully charged with a color mixed on the palette to achieve a dominant color area of the subject, (in this case part of the dark foliage), I lay it on as directly as possible.

Step 1

Step 2

Thick and Thin (Impasto)

Observe that I do not begin at the edge of the canvas, but rather near an area where several values, important to the picture, are in contrast. Also I do not continue to paint the same color area, but soon attempt to establish part of one of the other color values near the one started.

This procedure is continued. No attempt is made to finish each object, but rather to continue the process of setting up relationships — one color area to another. A concentrated effort is made to let each brush stroke be the last for the area it covers. This is the essence of *alla prima* painting. The dark areas are applied with sufficient paint to cover, but in the light areas a conscientious effort is made to load on heavier paint, the thickest in the lightest spots. The impasto responds to the impact of the revelation of forms by light.

Step 4

Color Mixtures

The color I mixed for any given part of the painting, as shown in the foregoing steps, was based on a strong sense of response to the subject, but not an exact matching of colors. I hesitate to state formulas because I feel they may be too rigid and misleading, and because I do not mix colors by that thought process. I play the palette as one might play the piano by ear. The exact value of the color is uppermost in my mind and the thermal (warmth or coolness of the color) is next. Different combinations of pigments will often serve.

For the dark parts of the foliage and vase, shown in step 2, I used a mixture of Ultramarine Blue, Burnt Sienna, and a little Alizarin Crimson. For the light parts of the peonies I used mostly White with varying additions of Alizarin Crimson, Yellow Ochre, Cadmium Red, Cadmium Yellow, Indian Red, also tiny bits of Cobalt Blue and Viridian. For the shadowy parts of the Peonies I used Cobalt Blue, Yellow Ochre, Indian Red, and a little Viridian and White. Within the framework of *values* and *thermal* I could have used a different assortment of colors without disturbing the illusion of the picture. The precise color used should be a response to the artist's sense of taste rather than an attempt to "match" the color of something in nature.

In combining colors it is not necessary to mix the colors thoroughly on the palette. In fact too much mixing deadens the color, just as excessive brushing or smoothing on the canvas does. Leave some of the mixing for the eye of the beholder — it is more exciting.

In the close-up above, the individual brush strokes can be seen. They are the handwriting of the artist. They cannot be "practiced" like elementary penmanship, but must be a natural and unselfconcious development resulting from the artists drive to set down what he wishes with all the speed and sureness he can command.

Spring Flowers

4

LET'S TRY A LANDSCAPE

Additional Equipment

Landscape painting requires special equipment but, in this age of the automobile, one does not have to be as exacting about lightness and portability as in Turner's day. Still, it is seldom possible to drive right to the spot where you wish to set up your easel, so due consideration should be given to equipment.

A stool is a great convenience, and several lightweight, folding types are on the market. Sargent always surrounded himself with umbrellas to ward off sun and wind. This was in the carriage era, but it was also in an age of available servants. Personally, I like the sun, and wind presents no real problem if your easel has its legs well planted and your canvas is not too large. Sand blowing onto your palette can be annoying, so can insects (a bottle of insect repellent in the paint box is helpful), small children and natives (both friendly and otherwise) are among other difficulties that may plague the landscapist. All is not hazard, however. The reward can be very great.

There is no deeper satisfaction than carrying off a good sketch. Even a poor one is fun — scraping the canvas clean afterward has its own pleasurable sensation of achievement. With a couple of boon companions, the close of day on a sketching trip is joy unrefined — not even hunting and fishing can touch it.

Some people are very clever about gadgets. A friend of mine has a tiny, battery powered light rigged for night sketching. Another friend had a jacket made with special pockets for various sketching tools. Many things may suggest themselves — just don't overburden yourself.

Perspective

Perspective, like anatomy, is an involved subject in itself. Like anatomy, it is a necessary part of an artist's studies, especially when we consider the landscape, but the beginner need not wait until he *knows* these subjects before he delves into color and creative painting. In fact, it is no doubt possible to paint important pictures with little knowledge of either. The scope of this book will not permit a full treatment of the subject (some recommended books are listed in the Bibliography), but we will touch upon elementary or "sketchers'" perspective.

The first point that must be grasped is the "eye level" concept. The eye level is the horizon, the true horizon. It is the line where sky and water meet when you look out over a large body of water. But it is there, whether it forms a visible line or not. It accompanies you like your shadow. It is simply a flat plane on the level of your eyes.

Picture an imaginary liquid, like water, flooding the world about you, up to the level of your eyes, (if you feel you are drowning, imagine yourself a snorkel for breathing purposes). Whether you stand or sit, imagine this water level rising or falling so that it is always at the level of your eyes. Where this water level laps against the wall across the room, or against houses, or tree trunks, or whatever, is the location of the eye level at the limit of your vision. When you draw the line on your paper remember that it is an imaginary line at infinity and is not part of the picture, unless it happens to be the natural horizon — as at sea.

Most things built by man, buildings, furniture, and so forth, have many lines in their construction that are level — or parallel to the surface of the earth. This is convenient for the study of perspective because these lines, if extended, converge at the eye level line. Any group of lines that are parallel to each other converge at the same point on the eye level line. This is called the "vanishing point." To find this vanishing point for any group of parallel lines that are also parallel to the surface of the earth, as in a house, or table, proceed as follows: imagine a line starting from where you are, and proceeding in a direction *parallel* with the set of parallel lines you are concerned with. A good way to do this is to point, as though aiming a pistol. The point at which this new line meets the eye level line is the vanishing point you seek.

By sighting and measuring (with your brush handle) you can determine how far this vanishing point should be from the object you are drawing, in terms of the scale you have established.

Lines that are parallel to each other but are *not* parallel to the surface of the earth, (the sloping lines of a roof, etcetera) also have a vanishing point. It is not on our eye level line, however, but is in the plane these lines are parallel to. Also, shapes that are irregular, such as boats, rocks, and even clouds, can be considered from a perspective standpoint by imagining them simplified into "regular" box-like shapes so you can locate their vanishing points.

Very often the vanishing point will prove to be well off the limits of your drawing. When this happens indoors you can put your drawing board on the floor, and with a thumb tack at the vanishing point, stretch a length of string to extend the lines. For general sketching purposes, however, such elaborate precision is not necessary. It is usually only necessary to get the "sense" of the perspective aspect of the subject to make a successfully workable drawing.

A word of caution, based on observation of errors frequently made by beginners: be careful not to overemphasive perspective effect in lines *near* the eye level. By the same token, do not understate perspective effect, well above — or below — eye level.

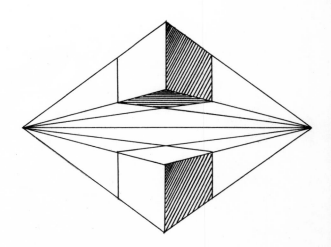

Finding the vanishing point.

The vanishing point of an irregular shaped object.

Choosing a Subject

It was once deemed necessary for English landscape painters to hie themselves off to Italy in search of appropriate subjects. Constable, perhaps the greatest of them all, decided it was not necessary to go more than a few steps from his cottage — proving conclusively that one's backyard can be inspiring.

Pissaro said of landscape painting that the principal thing was to "... establish the accord between the sky and earth." The changing sky is always present, and while trips are nice, they are not essential to the search for subjects. In fact, a valid argument could be advanced that the reverse is true. Often, on a trip one sees more with the tourists' eye than with the artists'. The "breath-taking view" demands the attention. The lure of the next turn in the road is irresistible. In familiar surroundings the humble and commonplace may reveal to us the deepest and most stirring inspiration.

Study the great painters and turn a receptive eye to the world around. Using the viewfinder, described on page 11, can help. A couple of trees and a patch of sky was sufficient for Gainsborough or Troyon. The back porch was good enough for Liebermann. The aging Monet painted his lily pool over and over, finding fresh delight in each changing aspect.

The Need for Speed

In painting landscape on the spot, speed is of the essence. The light changes, and with the changing light the subject vanishes; for the raw material of pictures is not inherent in things, but in their *aspect*. The impulse to which one responds in starting a painting, can best be sustained while the aspect remains somewhat constant. After two or three hours, the light has so shifted that one is hard put to recall the mood. It is preferable to return the next day at the same hour, or to finish entirely from memory, rather than to continue to refer to a subject in which the aspect is completely altered.

Several things will assist in developing speed. The most obvious is practice; also work-ing in a fairly small size. Perhaps the real key to speed, as well as to the profound heart of the whole of painting, is to *see* the subject in its essential and fundamental form. Details must be subordinated to the whole. There is nothing wrong with detail, so long as it meets this requirement. Simplification is another key to artistic unity. If two adjacent tones are nearly the same, they may be considered as one — whether they are the same or entirely different substances. There is nothing gained by straining to show separation in contiguous areas that are the same in value. Unification, on the other hand, can strengthen the design and achieve an evocation of the mood with speed and sureness.

Step 1

Step 2

Step 3

Block in a landscape roughly with char-coal (page 49). Accent the details with pencil and begin painting directly in full color with a loaded brush. Fill in each area with its color. Do not smooth out the paint or "go over" if you can avoid it. Re-member — speed is essential. Proceed with some of the strong darks (as below).

Step 4

Fill in the areas — like a jig saw puzzle. In mixing the colors remember that the value is paramount. When you've filled in all the areas the picture should be practically complete. Minor corrections and details such as small figures or distant boats can be put in last or may be added back in the studio.

Step 5

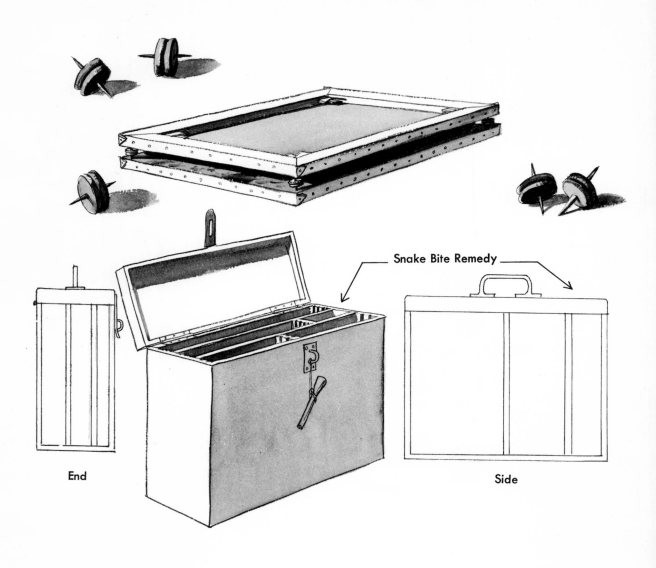

Snake Bite Remedy

End

Side

Wet Paint (Transporting Sketches)

I mentioned earlier that working outdoors in small size helped achieve speed. There are other practical advantages to working in "thumb box" size. Oil paintings do not dry for several days and it's easier to store and handle small wet paintings than large ones. I sometimes do a 16 x 20 on the spot but most often my favorite sizes are 8 x 10 to 12 x 16 inches. The lid of my paint box has grooves in which three 12 x 16 inch panels can be carried while wet. I also have a box similarly grooved for carrying four 8 x 10's, 10 x 14's, and 12 x 16's. Canvas pins to separate wet paintings (see sketch) are ready at hand in my paint box.

Manor Park, Larchmont

This little sketch (10 x 14) was painted in about an hour and a half late on a July afternoon. The mood of the picture was established in the first few minutes by the painting of the sky (page 50). All the rest really serves as a foil for the sky. A couple of the figures were actually observed and sketched in in the last few moments. They were strengthened and others added back in the studio.

5

DOWN TO THE SEA

About Reflections

The painting of water revolves mainly around an understanding of the phenomenon of reflections. "The angle of incidence equals the angle of reflection." The angle involved between the artist's eye and any given spot on the water is the same as the angle between that spot and whatever is reflected in the water. In short, the surface of water acts as a mirror. The clearer and more still the water, the more perfect the mirror effect. When water is disturbed by waves, its reflecting surface can be likened to a mirror that has been glued to a cloth backing, and then shattered into many little pieces. If this broken mirror is placed face upward on the ground, and its cloth backing made to resemble waves, the small fractured bits of mirror will then act somewhat in the manner of the irregular facets of a wave. Different parts of the wave reflect different parts of the sky, or whatever else happens to be in a position to be reflected. Generally, the slope of a wave nearest you reflects the upper part of the sky while that part of the wave sloping down the far side, toward the trough, will reflect areas of sky nearer the horizon. Since the sky is usually a different color and value in its different quarters, different colors and values are imparted to the water rippling beneath it. Also, no matter what other objects, such as boats, trees, or hills, are in a position to be reflected, the sky will still have a dominant effect on the general color of the water because of its vastness. The color of the

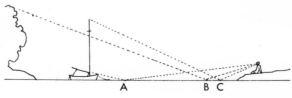

Points at which different parts of the scene are reflected to the eye.

A. The boat hull and cover.
B. The trees on the far shore.
C. The boat's mast.

bottom in shallow water, and the darkness of the depths, will influence the color where those facets of waves are tilted at an angle to the eye so that the sight can penetrate.

Water, of course, is not a perfect mirror, because it is not perfectly clear and colorless. Some water has algae or silt in suspension which gives it a characteristic color. This local color of the water tends to modify and reduce the color reflected by its surface. If enough sediment is present, as in a very muddy river, the reflecting power of the water is reduced to a minimum and its appearance then is more that of an opaque glossy substance, like a table top. Shadows may be cast on such water (do not confuse these with reflections). Another generally reliable rule is that the reflection is darker than the color reflected.

The sea is a mirror.

Combinations of shadows and reflections.

Quick Sketches of Surf

Pastels are good for rapid sketches of moving water. Little equipment is needed and the sketch can be used for translation into oil or watercolor. The method is described on page 60.

Analyzing Appearances

The more inquiring and analytical one's approach to the appearance of things, the better. The study of nature, from the artist's point of view, is not the same as the scientist's, but there is a relationship — a searching for truth. This analytical approach applies with particular force to the painting of moving and changing shapes, such as clouds or surf.

The rolling sea captures the imagination as no other element. It lends itself to infinitely varied interpretation. It evokes — and responds to — many moods. Let us consider further the fundamentals of its appearance.

The restless waters, driven by wind or other force, surge forward and upward and burst the bonds of surface tension. The glassy, mirror-like surface is suddenly transformed. A dancing white plume appears. The tumbling water, rolling forward, is filled with millions of bubbles which roll and toss ahead of the driving force. The massed bubbles reflect all of the light and produce the short-lived dazzling whiteness. The heaving surface that released the bubbles soon reclaims them. As they disperse, and settle, and trail behind the brilliant climax of their birth, the enveloping unbroken water diminishes their brightness, which gives way to a milky green. This lovely jade color lingers for a moment, like a dying candle, then it, too, vanishes. This process, endlessly repeated, with the boundless profligacy of nature, creates a superb ballet on any breezy afternoon.

The waves rushing shoreward pile up as shoaling water confines them and crash upon sand or rocks, with many repetitions of the white and green, in the surge and counter-surge of mighty force.

Nature and Imagination

Can this drama be "copied" in line and color? It is certainly a restless model. I think the answer is that it must be observed and the phenomenon of its action re-created in the imagination. It has been said that the artist does his best work from imagination; but this is like a bank account, in that you can only take out as much as you have put in. Observation of nature is the way to make deposits.

Painting the restless sea, or other violent action, clearly enforces the need to store information and experience, and to reassemble and synthesize it in the imagination. This principle applies also to more static subjects, however, for in the alembic of the mind, art takes its form.

Can the Camera Sketch?

One might say of all this, "why not take a snap-shot?" and to be sure, this simple logic is often practiced. It is not always understood, however, that this mechanical aid can also be a serious roadblock. It is manifestly true that the invention of the camera has greatly increased the ease of picture making, but there is no evidence that it has ever, or ever will,

contribute anything to the art. Perhaps it has taken more away than it has given. In any case, the student must recognize that in using photographs he is imposing a mechanical device between his eye and nature. The camera does not "see" in the same way that he does.

The human eye focuses on only one pin point at a time. The camera focuses more or less equally from right to left, and top to bottom, of its field of vision. No thought or emotion is involved in the camera's "seeing," and only a modicum of personality can be imparted through the skill of the photographer.

Photographs of things in violent motion (where the camera should, logically, be most useful), are poorer artistically than of things at rest, because of the frozen appearance of the motion. This especially applies to moving water. Great skill is required to interpret the information provided by photographs to make them useful to the painter. It seems almost axiomatic that so much skill and knowledge are required to make proper use of them that one so skilled finds little need.

The great realist, Pietro Annigoni, says of the camera in this regard that ". . . it can produce only feebly the appearances of nature and life. For this reason it does not interest me even as a means. A hasty sketch set down under the impulse of a spontaneous emotion of my own is for me a thousand times more vital and evocative."

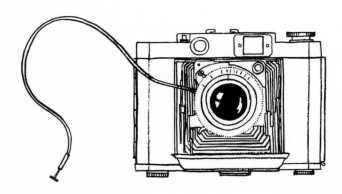

A sketch in charcoal, or other black and white media, can be used as a basis for painting in the studio. The values established in black and white provide enough information to experiment in color. A good photograph provides the same information but with far less sensitivity and with a mechanical, rather than a human, response to the subject.

Written notes on the sketch or margin of the paper can be useful, particularly if they help recall the warmth or coolness involved. A mere recording of local colors is of little use as these can be altered at will to suit your wishes. The values and the thermal are of paramount importance.

Painting on the Rocks

Black and white drawings of the surf, done on the spot, can provide a fine means of study, as well as a great deal of material for future pictures.

Another method I have found that is fast and effective is to make color studies in pastel (page 56). For this work, I carefully select a limited number of pastel chalks and a colored paper of a tone that will supply one of the values. I try to select one pastel for each of the remaining, dominant color values: one for the light portion of the white water; one for the shadows on the white; another for the green aerated part; and perhaps two for the clear water. One or two darker sticks, for rock forms, completes the outfit.

Armed with this simple equipment, and working in small size, I can rapidly set down color notes of permanent usefulness.

In making an oil sketch on the spot, I use somewhat the same approach as with the pastels. That is, I work in small size with only a few brushes and colors.

Back in the studio a larger painting nearly always follows a small study that seemed to "go" well. Sometimes, a considerable span, even years, transpires between the two. Usually some changes in composition or effect are incorporated in the larger painting — not always to its advantage. The larger painting generally takes much longer than the sketch, even though it may not seem any more complex — often it is simpler. In the studio, one has time to mull over the various colors and areas. The difficult thing is to retain the spontaneity and freshness of the original study.

This drawing of surf and the one on the preceding page show the great difference in appearance brought about by a variation in the direction and kind of light involved. White water is not necessarily white in value.

"Homer's Return"

It is said that Winslow Homer, one of the greatest marine painters of all time, often took his studio paintings of surf—even large ones— back to the location of the subject for final touches. I have tried this on occasion and consider it an excellent practice. After much pondering and soul searching over a certain passage of your painting in the studio, very often the solution comes easily and clearly in the smiling face of nature.

The view finder helps to concentrate the field of vision in selecting a "surf and rock" composition. So much excitement is generated by such a scene that one has difficulty in choosing. Don't try to take in too much. Try to avoid being dominated in your thinking by the action of the rolling surf. Most often, in this type of subject, the dominant effect is the light pattern of the sea and sky, on the one hand, opposed by the darker rocks, on the other. Be careful to select a spot that is reasonably safe from the rising tide or that occasional extra big wave — "widow makers" — in the parlance of the sea.

The charcoal drawing established the pattern of the main elements of the picture. A few rough shadings helped to distinguish between light and dark areas. The particular moment of sea motion was also decided at this time and roughed in. The sea is a restless model but she does assume nearly the same pose over and over. Make sure you allow sufficient timing between various wave actions shown. Remember that the receding surge of one breaker builds up and causes the next. Don't try to show too many. Winslow Homer used to say three was plenty.

After spraying on a little fixative, to secure the charcoal, the second step shown was begun. The relationship between sky and sea was established with broad strokes of color mixed on the palette. White, Ultramarine Blue, and Indian Red made the pearly gray of the misty lower sky. The same color mixture, with more blue and a little Yellow Ochre added, produced the distant sea. The horizon, at times nearly lost in the sea haze, was blended into the sky with horizontal strokes.

Patches of foam were heaved upward by the advancing wave and provided a pattern for describing the wave. In the lower illustration the dark patterns of the rock masses were established. The shadows in the rocks, composed of Ultramarine Blue, Burnt Sienna, and a little Alizarin Crimson, are cool and almost black in intensity. The sun-lit part of the rocks is warm. Indian Red, Yellow Ochre, Burnt Sienna, dominate, but with blue, Viridian and White added where wet rocks glisten coolly in the slanting light.

A fine crashing surf provided by hurricane "Daisy" passing to seaward built up as the sketch progressed, as shown in the upper photo. Shadows in the white of the breaking wave were blocked in with White, Ultramarine Blue, Indian Red and a bit of Yellow Ochre. The green "back" of the curling breaker is principally Yellow Ochre, Viridian and White. A similar mixture provides the color for patches in the churning white water in the foreground. The brightest part of the latter area, and the sun-lit parts of the white breaker are heavily painted with White, tinted with Cadmium Yellow Pale, Cadmium Red, and Alizarin Crimson.

The two lower illustrations show the finishing touches. "Holidays" filled in; edges softened, here and there, and a distant comber emphasized.

The color plate of the finished sketch (opposite) is a souvenir of a delightful morning spent at "The Ledges," the Newport estate of Howard G. Cushing.

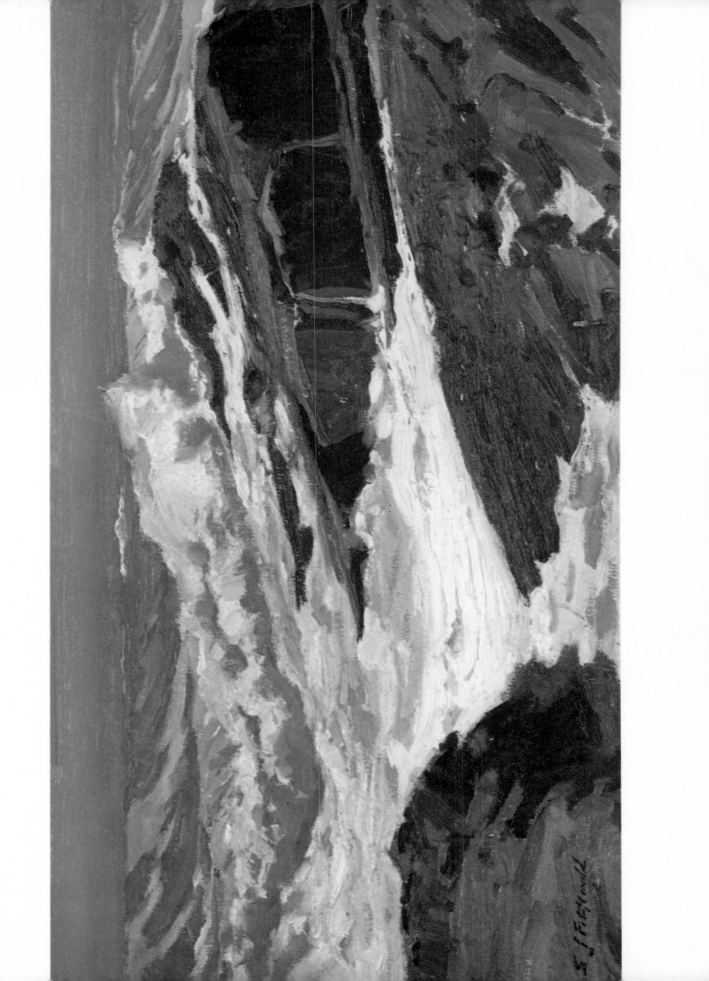

The Ledges

THE PREPARED APPROACH

More on Composition

In a way, composition is the end product of all the various parts of an artist's training. When we learn something about proportion, light and shade, perspective, and color, we are confronted with the problem of how to combine these interesting tools.

Actually, we began composing with the first line drawn — even earlier — because the mental picture is the start of composition.

The paintings of children have tremendous impact because the child is unhampered by means. He drives to the heart of the matter in his insistence to establish the picture. With him, the "picture is the thing" — to paraphrase a principle from the art of drama.

Elaborate systems have been devised to analyze pictorial composition or to assist in composing by method. These systems are interesting to study, the Bibliography lists some sources. My own conviction is that too close an application of such methods causes more confusion than good and gets in the way of, rather than assists, personal expression.

What makes a "good" composition, in the final analysis, depends on whether you like it or not. In short, it involves taste, which is the sum total of much more than training in the mechanics of art. It involves the total person.

The study of nature and the great paintings readily available in books and museums, and a tiny soupçon of confidence about what you like is, to me, the best recipe for "How to Compose Pictures."

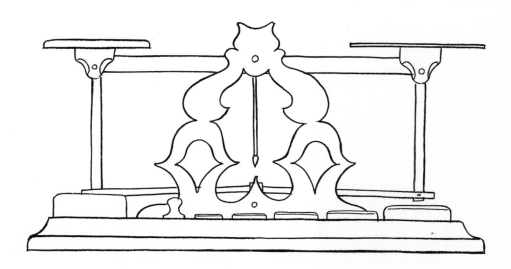

BOUGIE, ALGERIA

GREENWICH VILLAGE, N.Y.

The sketches on this and the next page are notes taken at various times and places to explore picture possibilities seen in nature. They are not so much studies of things (although they serve that purpose too), but of compositional arrangements.

LARCHMONT, N.Y.

Note in these sketches that the direction of light and other circumstances of the moment play an important part in the picture arrangement. The sketches are records of a chance visual experience, but it should be noted that — even so — some objects were left out or shifted a bit in the sketching to enhance the effect.

"UTAH BEACH", NORMANDY

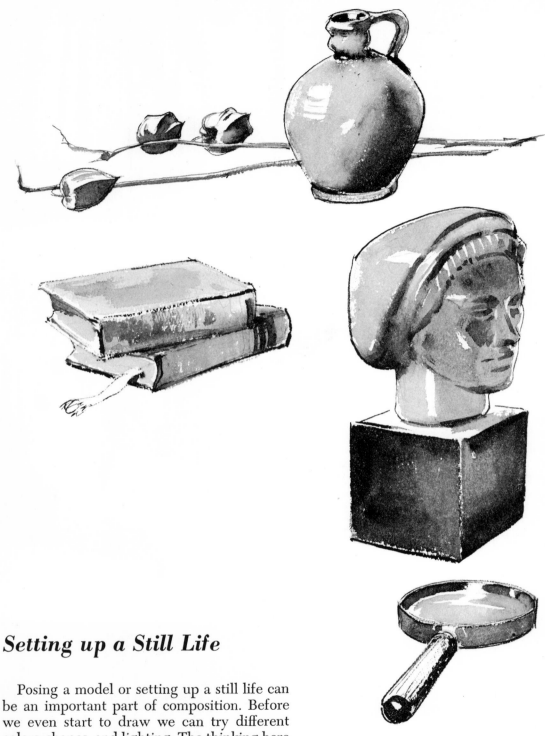

Setting up a Still Life

Posing a model or setting up a still life can be an important part of composition. Before we even start to draw we can try different colors, shapes, and lighting. The thinking here is similar to that concerned with decorating a room or choosing a costume. The main difference, of course, is that our arrangement is to be enclosed in the boundaries of a frame, to make a picture. Here the view-finder can be of help.

1

The group of objects shown on the preceding page were tried in various arrangements to set up a still-life subject. Many possibilities suggested themselves. A few are shown here.

2

Arrangements number one and two seemed too scattered and lacking in focal point or center of interest. After shifting the objects this way and that, it was decided that a dark background might be better. A piece of black velvet drapery proved most satisfying.

3

The black background made a strong contrast with the objects on the marble top table, and I began to feel that I was on the right track. With a little more shifting I arrived at the grouping which was developed into the painting shown in the succeeding pages.

Underpainting

Heretofore, only *alla prima* painting has been considered. Another method that was used by many of the old masters can be termed a "grisaille and glaze" method. The purpose of this method is to separate the problems of painting into parts.

The grisaille is an underpainting in gray, in which the modelling of the values is completed first. When it has dried, the color is applied in glazes of sufficient transparency so that the underlying values assert themselves. Thus, one can concentrate on the color problem somewhat separately from the value problem — Napoleon's dictum of "divide and conquer." I cannot pretend there are no "Waterloo's" here, but it is a method that has fascinating possibilities.

The underpainting can be done in one dark pigment and white. My favorite is Raw Umber for this. It is sufficiently neutral, and is fast drying. Terre Verte is also good and other possibilities offer areas for experimentation.

The white used for the underpainting merits particular attention. My preference is white lead ground in linseed oil. Winsor and Newton supply such a white under the name of "Foundation White." White lead ground in poppy oil (Flake White or Cremnitz White) is rather slow drying as are Titanium or Zinc whites. Several color makers supply an underpainting white described as "containing no lead," but fast drying. While these are a little faster drying than the lead, I find them far less malleable and pleasant working. White lead is ideally suited to underpainting as it dries rapidly to a tough, flexible film. It is the "leanest" of all pigments and thus ensures compliance with the ancient principle of "fat over lean." It is the white of the Old Masters.

In the underpainting, one's efforts can be concentrated on all elements of the picture except color. The darks should be painted rather thinly, the lights, more heavily, and great care can be exercised in developing the modelling. When the underpainting is finished the appearance is somewhat that of a photograph of the finished painting. In portrait painting, or similar commission, this is a good point to permit the client a look at the work. The grisaille should be well dried before glazing.

Step 1

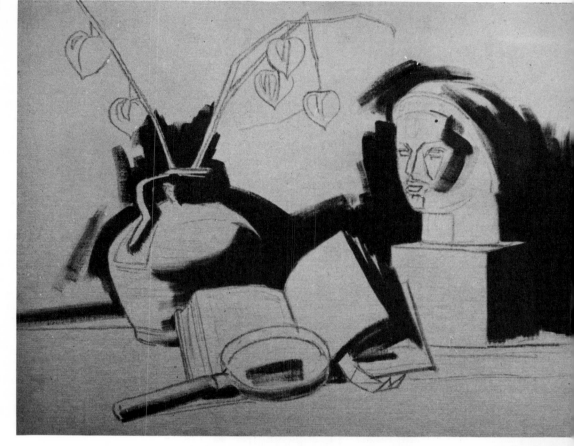

After completing the drawing, opposite page, I began the underpainting with Foundation White (white lead ground in linseed oil) and a single dark pigment, Raw Umber. As usual, I started with an area of dominant color near the center of interest (above). Proceeding as in alla prima painting, I related one value to another and expanded in this way to all parts of the picture (below). Since at this stage one is not concerned with color, every effort can be concentrated on the value pattern of the picture, and textures and forms can be studied fully.

Glazing

For glazing, special attention must be given to the medium. More medium is required than in *alla prima* painting, as the colors must be thinned to permit the underpainting to function. Too much linseed oil is not desirable, as it is too "runny" and would cause yellowing. Much experimenting is possible in the choice of a medium. I generally use a glaze medium composed of:

One part Damar Varnish
One part Stand Oil
Three to five parts Turpentine

Sable brushes are usually more satisfactory for glazing than bristle, especially in smaller areas. Areas of continuous color should be covered in continuous operations. Color changes can be incorporated as the glaze is applied and it is possible to work into wet glazes. Evaporation of the turpentine and the presence of the varnish causes the glaze to become "tacky" fairly soon. Several glazes can be superimposed as the underlying glaze becomes dry. Care should be exercised to use less turpentine in the upper glazes. This is in accord with the principle of "fat over lean." The reason being that a fast drying paint applied over a slow drying one may cause cracking. A little white may be mixed with the glazes. For this the slower drying poppy-oil whites, such as Flake, Zinc or Titanium are preferable to the lead-in-linseed-oil white used for the underpainting.

Strictly speaking, a glaze is always darker than the tone it is applied over. It is possible to apply, in an operation similar to glazing, a tone somewhat lighter than the underlying passage. This is called "scumbling." Very beautiful atmospheric effects can be achieved by scumbling. Too much reliance on this procedure tends to produce an appearance of weakness and indecision, however, and it therefore should be used with restraint.

In the final phase of the grisaille and glaze method small strokes of heavy impasto may be applied, such as high lights. Great charm and "paint quality" can be achieved by the use of these touches in the variety and added dimension they impart, contrasting, as they do, in texture with the underlying glazes.

The photograph opposite was taken of the completed underpainting. When the underpainting was dry, and before glazing, it was given a coat of retouch varnish to isolate the underpainting from the glazes. This prevents unequal absorbency of the glazes by the thick and thin parts of the underpainting.

The reproduction opposite shows the partly glazed painting. The brownish-gray of the underpainting is only partly covered. The painting procedure is not too different from the direct method discussed in earlier chapters, except that the colors are applied more thinly (using the glaze medium) and the grisaille provides a strong textural guide for the color.

Still Life

Grisaille and glaze stages

Still Life

PORTRAITS

Special Problems

Someone has said that portrait painting is the most difficult form of commercial art.

It is not commercial art in the usual sense, but it has an element in common with commercial art: the requirement to perform a special function — in addition to artistic requirements — which makes it a most difficult and exacting art. The requirement is that it must resemble the sitter.

At times, perhaps, this requirement is pressed too far, either by the sitter or the artist, so that a loss of artistic quality results. It does not matter now whether Rembrandt's portraits looked like the sitter or not. Naturally it mattered a great deal to the sitter when it was done. It is manifestly true, however, that the most important consideration in a portrait, or any other work of art, is its artistic quality and integrity. A curious thing about likeness is that if you strain too hard to capture it, it may escape you entirely—like trying to pet a shy kitten—pay elaborate attention to every-

thing else and it will fall into your lap.

The features (eyes, nose, and mouth) are, after all, only a small part of the head. Concentration on the forms surrounding and underlying the features will usually contribute more to likeness than tickling away, and cat-licking with a little brush, at the features.

Anatomy

A knowledge of anatomy is essential to an understanding of portraiture in its profound aspects. However, very creditable amateur painting has been done in this field with only a superficial knowledge of the skeleton and muscles, and their workings.

The scope of this book will not permit more than a glance at this subject (some recommended books are in the Bibliography). A few drawings are inserted here to serve as an introduction to this fascinating subject, and as a guide through some of the more obvious anatomical problems.

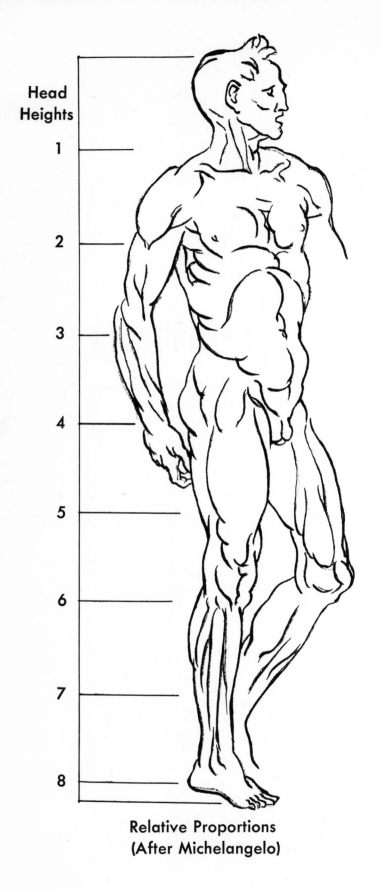

**Head
Heights**

1

2

3

4

5

6

7

8

Relative Proportions
(After Michelangelo)

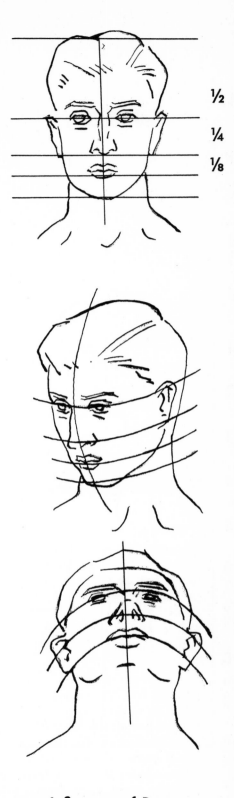

½

¼

⅛

Influence of Perspec-
tive on Proportions

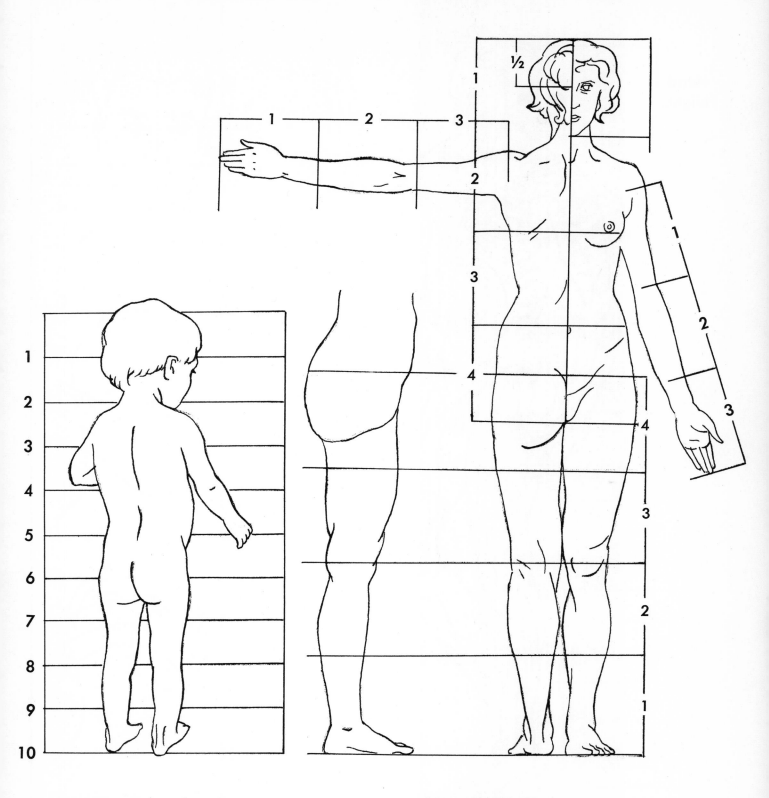

**Proportions of a child
(After Kollmann)**

**Relative Proportions
as given by Richer**

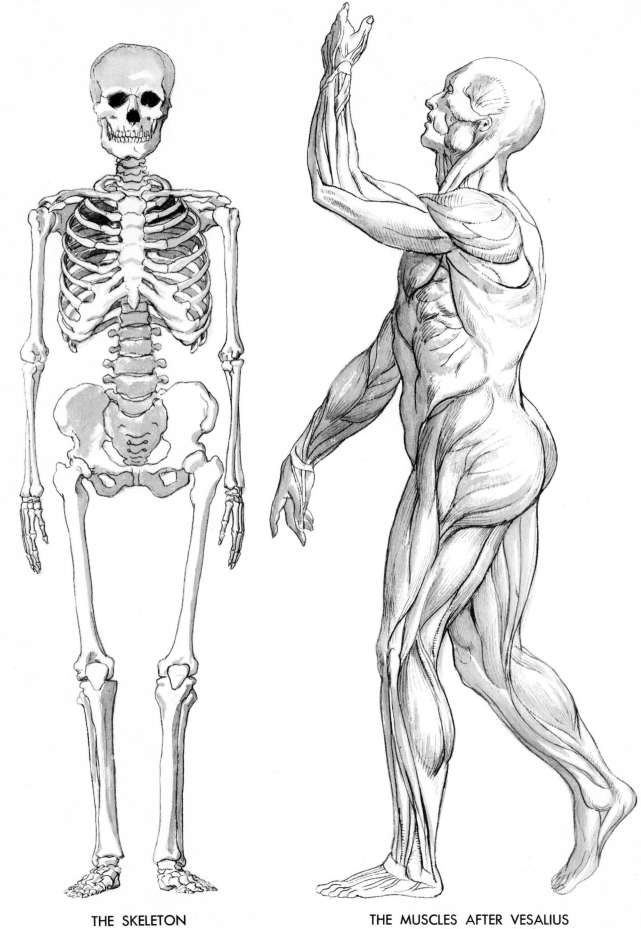

THE SKELETON   THE MUSCLES AFTER VESALIUS

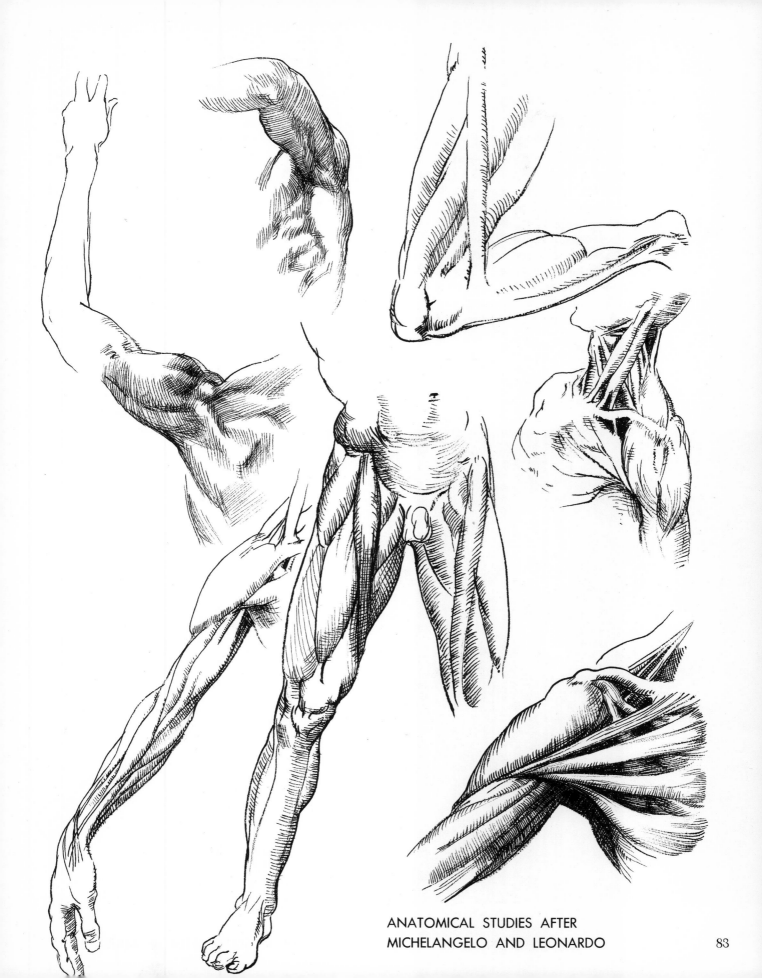

ANATOMICAL STUDIES AFTER
MICHELANGELO AND LEONARDO

83

Sitter Reaction

Different sitters respond differently to the whole project of portraiture — as do different artists. Some portrait painters rig a mirror so the sitter can watch the progress of the work. Others have a standing rule that the portrait may not be viewed until a time he considers suitable. Occasionally a sitter does not wish to see the work until finished. It is very hard to make rules that will properly suit all occasions and temperaments. The important thing to bear in mind is that everyone concerned is interested in getting the best possible portrait.

All steps taken should lead to that end. This principle applies to professional and amateur alike.

Generally, I feel it is an unnecessary denial to the sitter to withhold viewing of the work during the painting. I do not hesitate to do so, however, if it seems that the end result will be better for it. I think it is best to discuss this frankly with the sitter beforehand, decide on a procedure, and stick to it. A feeling of warmth, mutual respect, and cooperation between painter and sitter helps to produce a better portrait.

Pose and Background

The same principles apply to arrangement of subject in portraiture as in still life. The artist must try to look upon the major divisions of color value — background, flesh tones, costume — as patterns enclosed in a frame, and thus forming a picture. Again the view-finder helps. In arranging the pose, a limiting factor that must be considered is the comfort of the sitter. A pose that is too strained is bad for both sitter and painter.

A plain wall, or a piece of drapery, makes the simplest background. One can thus easily control the selection of a color that fits into the abstract pattern of the picture. Landscape, or objects significant to the activities and character of the subject, may be used. Care must be taken to keep such items subordinate to the main theme — the sitter. In this the lighting can be of help.

Lighting

Most portrait painters prefer a natural north light from a skylight or a window placed rather high in the room. North light remains more constant through a longer part of the day because it does not involve direct sunlight. Shafts of sunlight may be dramatic, but are too transitory. The high source of light coming down to the model at about 45 degrees most easily concentrates the light on the head and upper part

Be sure the pose is reasonably comfortable. Discuss number of sittings, rests, viewing of work by sitter or family, and all similar problems with the client before starting work.

of the body, thus helping the main theme of concentration of effect upon the head in the picture.

Draperies or screens can be useful in causing areas of the subject, either the person or surroundings, to be in shadow or subdued light.

In the absence of a regular studio window, a fairly tall window with the lower part blocked by cardboard is a good substitute. If possible select a window which, from the sitters position, reveals only sky. This will help avoid changing and disturbing reflected lights thrown back by buildings, trees, and so forth.

Artificial light is far more controllable than daylight, and artists often use it. There is something about the light that falls over the

form from the vast distance of the sky that is infinitely finer, however. Avoid the hazard of starting a subject under one condition of light and working further under an entirely different one.

If you must use photographs (and they can be helpful to supplement limited sittings) take them yourself, or direct their taking, with the sitter in the position and under conditions of lighting you have decided upon for the painting. Use no other lights (the photographer will probably want to). Avoid — like the plague — using the usual portrait photographer's prints to work from — or photographs taken by flash. The artificiality of this type of lighting is fine in the mechanical medium of photography, but has nothing to contribute to painting.

Step 1

Painting Procedure

The process of painting a portrait should be very similar to the painting of other subject matter. One of the worst hazards of the special problem of portrait painting — the likeness requirement — is that it confronts you like a bad conscience. If you can tackle the problem with the somewhat detached attitude you would apply to a still-life, you will produce a better portrait.

The method of painting this portrait was the grisaille and glaze method described in Chapter 6. The three steps shown here demonstrate stages in the development of the grisaille underpainting.

Step 2

Step 3

Janis

REAR ADMIRAL THOMAS J. ROBBINS,
United States Navy

The portraits on this, the preceding, and the next page are all done in the grisaille and glaze method. This "Old Master" method has great possibilities, particularly in the careful, more finished type of work generally required in portraiture.

Ryder

(Overleaf)

BUILDING A MURAL

The purpose of this chapter is to enlarge upon the theme of assembling material from various sources in order to construct a picture. The subject — mural painting — involves principles that also apply to story illustration and advertising art, as well as picture making in general.

Mural painting is a large subject, and no attempt will be made here to cover it fully. A particular mural is used as an example of a problem and its solution, that will have application to other artistic problems.

The Problem

The problem was to design, and paint, a mural for the lobby of the Seamen's Church Institute in New York, as a tribute to the 6,000 merchant seamen who lost their lives in World War II. The space assigned to the mural was a 40 x 10 foot wall area, extending from the top of a marble wainscoting to the ceiling, along a wall opposite the room's main entrance. Large supporting columns in the room prevented an uninterrupted view of the mural.

No theme was specified, so after due consideration, I fixed upon the Invasion of Normandy as an appropriate symbol of the great contribution to the war effort made by the men of the Merchant Marine. Of all the great operations of the war involving men and ships of the merchant fleet, D-day at Normandy — the greatest waterborne invasion of history — expressed their vital part in the victory most completely. Also, I happened to have been there.

Perusal of my sketch books, and some visualizing on the layout pad, (described in Chapter IX) and the general idea began to take shape; a view of the anchorage area off "Omaha" beach. The dominant ship pictured was to be an EC-2 type — the famous Liberty Ship — workhorse of the war.

The problem of the intervening columns was handled by creating three centers of interest to show between the columns.

The Sketch

A color sketch, in watercolor, one inch to the foot, or 40 x 10 inches, was developed and presented. In consultation with the architect, and others concerned with the project, some minor changes were suggested, including the addition of a life-boat in the foreground filled with merchant seamen. A line drawing was made, incorporating the suggested changes, which was then presented and approved.

More Comprehensive Sketch

The next step was the development of a one-fourth scale sketch. This was also done in outline on paper, 10 feet long by 2½ feet high. This stage afforded an opportunity to study many of the technical details of the ships. Many strolls along the waterfront, sketch book in hand, assisted in this task. Even at this scale, the figures involved were fairly small in this mural, so detailed study of the figures and their clothing was left for the next stage.

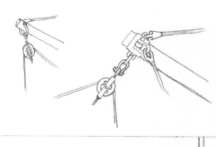

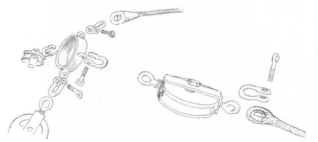

Full Scale Cartoon

The ten foot long sketch was next "squared off." This was done by dividing the length into 80 parts and the height into 20, and ruling the entire sketch into squares. Each square represented a 6 inch square in the full scale of 40 x 10 feet.

A full scale outline drawing was now made on paper prepared by marking it off in 6 inch squares. For convenience in handling, this was done on pieces of newsprint about 4 feet square, rather than a continuous 40 x 10 foot drawing. The enlarging was done by comparing the squares and drawing the forms correspondingly larger. Some additional research into technical detail was necessary at this time. I knew that my audience at the Seamen's Institute would be disconcerted if nautical details were not fully descriptive and accurate. Also, all the larger figures required special study. Models were obtained and drawings were made for each of the figures.

Most of the models were recruited from among the guests at the Institute. They were merchant seamen ashore for a spell between ships, and, like seafaring men the world over, a colorful and salty crowd, with a ready wit and time for a yarn. Watching television is tame fare compared to the entertaining and instructive company I had while making sketches of those fine fellows. With the addition of a few items of costume, some of them "doubled in brass" as GI's, descending the cargo nets into boats waiting to take them into the battle raging on shore.

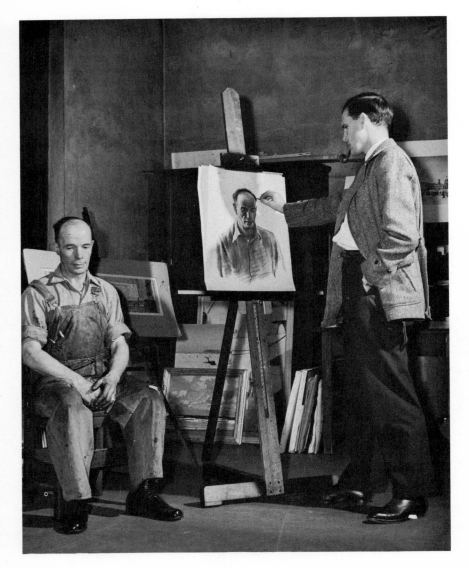

In mural work, as in story illustration or advertising art, the human figure usually plays an important part, and careful studies must be made for each figure. Professional models demand high fees and artists often use the camera to record the pose in order to shorten the posing time. If amateur models or friends can be used (as in the accompanying sketches) a more modest payment can usually be arranged. Sketching from life is infinitely finer than working from photographs (see Chapter 5).

Painting the Mural

Sometimes murals are done "in place," and this has distinct advantages in regard to achieving harmony with the surrounding architectural features, lighting, and so forth. Often a room is in constant use, or some other reason compels the painting of the mural elsewhere. This was the case at the Seamen's Institute.

A piece of heavy linen canvas was obtained, large enough for the mural. It was tacked flat to a temporary plywood wall, erected for the purpose. The canvas had been previously well primed with white, and the next step was the transferring of the drawing to the canvas from the full scale cartoon. This was done with the aid of large sheets of graphite carbon paper.

In mural work, the very long, straight lines needed to lay out the work are accomplished by means of the snap line. This is mason's twine, that can be stretched tightly between two nails driven in part way at predetermined points. A lump of colored chalk (usually blue) is then rubbed along the line. The line is then lifted a few inches, at a point midway between the two nails, and snapped back into position. A line is thus instantly "drawn" with the chalk, true and straight, between the nails.

When the drawing was on the canvas, painting was carried out in the most direct possible manner. No underpainting was used at all. The large areas such as sky, the large surfaces on the ships, and the water were painted, beginning at the top and working across and down the huge canvas. Small details were sometimes covered up, to be relocated later by means of the cartoon. Larger details were painted around and left to be filled in later.

Establishing the large values in their final state, right off, requires much visualizing because the white areas of canvas that still remain disturb the illusion of atmosphere and depth until they are painted in. Then the desired illusion enters in only if the first values are right! The brilliant effect of the white ground is lost, if a direct "one coat" painting is not achieved, particularly in the large areas. This requirement seems to me more compelling in large paintings than in small ones. I think it helps to account for the brilliance in the large works of Rubens.

By comparing the photograph below with the one on the preceding page, one can get an idea of the direct, alla prima method of painting used in this mural. The X-shaped device shown in the lower photograph is a proportional divider. It was made by tacking two sticks together at precisely the right point so that, when opened, the two ends form relative proportions one might wish to compare in enlarging. A drafting instrument of this type is made in a smaller size for drawing board work.

Seamen's Institute Mural

Seamen's Institute , New York
First Prize, National Society of Mural Painters, 1947

Adhesive is applied to the wall and the back of the canvas, which is then slowly unrolled into place. Every few feet a tack is applied at the upper edge to prevent sagging, as the lead adhesive dries slowly. Note the roller being used to smooth out bubbles. A lettered inscription five or six inches high was later installed on a separate strip of canvas along the bottom of the mural. Also, two decorative end strips were added. When these strips were added, to ensure a neat joining, the main canvas and the strips were trimmed at the same time with a straight edge and a sharp knife. The light fixture was replaced by flood lights for the mural.

Installing the Mural

The finished mural was secured with white lead. To accomplish this, a scaffold was built. The plaster wall was given a coat of shellac, after a couple of minor imperfections were treated with spackle. For convenience in moving the mural and preparing it for installation, it was rolled around a large cardboard tube with the painted surface in, which is contrary to the general rule for rolling paintings (see Chapter 10). The largeness of the roll, the flexibility of the fresh paint, and the need to have the back of the canvas exposed for the purpose of applying the adhesive, made infraction of the rule acceptable.

With the help of assistants, the ten foot roll was gradually unrolled into position, the adhesive being applied with a large paint brush to both the wall and the back of the canvas. The white lead was first prepared by stirring in damar varnish until a smooth — heavy cream — consistency was achieved. This makes an admirable adhesive for a large mural because it hardens slowly, permitting ample time to roll out any wrinkles or bubbles that may appear. It also obviates the dangers of shrinkage, inherent with adhesives in which water is present. The lead hardens to a rock-like consistency in time — a disadvantage if removal of a mural is ever anticipated.

After a few months of drying, the mural was given a light, even, coat of synthetic resin varnish to protect it from dirt. Every few years, or whenever necessary, this coating and the accumulated dust, can be removed with a mild solvent — turpentine or mineral spirits — and replaced.

Another example of the process of creating a picture for a specific purpose is illustrated by the sketch above. The problem was to design a mural for the boardroom of the White Laboratories. No theme was specified but a framed quotation from the great Louis Pasteur, observed in the office of the company's president suggested a starting point. A small pencil sketch produced encouraging results and after intensive research into the life of the great man, the above oil sketch, at a scale of two inches to the foot, was produced. The final mural (page 102) indicates some important changes in the design, notably a different treatment of the inscription, and a more accurate rendering of the chemical equipment used by Pasteur.

Louis Pasteur Mural

White Laboratories, Kenilworth, N. J.

TAKE INTEREST I IMPLORE YOU, IN THOSE SACRED DWELLINGS WHICH WE DESIGNATE
BY THE EXPRESSIVE TERM LABORATORIES. DEMAND THAT THEY BE MULTIPLIED
AND ADORNED. THEY ARE THE TEMPLES OF WELL-BEING AND HAPPINESS.
THERE IT IS THAT HUMANITY GROWS STRONGER, GREATER, BETTER.

L. Pasteur

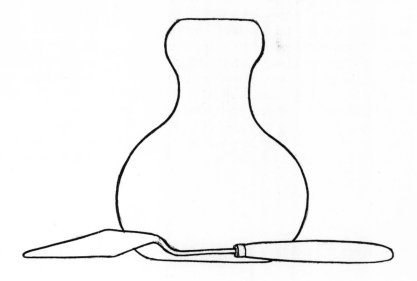

OTHER STUDIO PROJECTS

Developing Paintings From Sketches

Most paintings that finally arrive in frames and hang in exhibitions, or that are reproduced for illustrations, are developed as studio projects. It is seldom that a painting done in the open is complete and satisfying. There are exceptions to this rule, to be sure, and many of the "plein aire" painters and impressionists finish on the spot.

Illustrations or murals often require much research, and the assembling and organizing of material can be extremely interesting. It may even consume more time and effort than the painting itself.

Daumier is said to have arrived at the eloquent simplicity of his paintings by the process of making many tracings of his original sketch;

each successive tracing, perfecting, and simplifying the one before. Daumier, to be sure, is not the only one to avail himself of this simple but excellent procedure. Every art director and layout artist in the field of commercial art knows the value of the layout pad.

The layout pad is a sketch book, usually of large size, made up of sheets of tracing paper bound together. Normally, one works in this book on the last page first, working forward. In this way you can trace parts of the previous sketch. When you wish, it is easy to conceal the previous sketch simply by inserting a clean, opaque, sheet of paper. Also, it is easy to insert color sketches or drawings one wishes to develop or to abstract parts from them.

The Overlay

When a drawing is ready to transcribe to canvas or other painting surface one can apply soft pencil or graphite to the back, thus making a carbon paper. Large sheets of graphite carbon paper can also be purchased for this purpose. In transferring, be sure to secure the layout to the painting surface with thumb tacks or scotch tape to maintain correct register. In some complicated subjects it is well to keep this overlay fastened to the top edge of the canvas all during the painting. It can be folded back out of the way, but it is always available for ready reference.

Sometimes it is desirable to use an overlay that is more transparent than tracing paper; for instance, when a painting is in its final stage, and you are trying to decide whether to put in a figure or some other detail. A piece of glass or transparent acetate, can be placed over the painting and the detail painted on the transparent surface as a sort of "dry-run." If it looks right you can paint in the detail with more confidence than if you were trying it out on the original. If the original is still wet use glass rather than acetate, suspended above the wet canvas (acetate is not rigid enough).

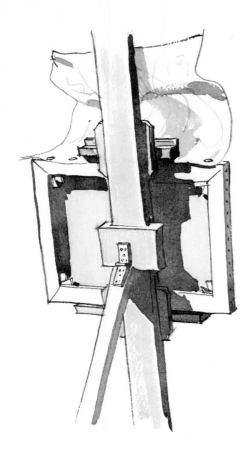

Various uses of an overlay are described in the text and illustrated in the accompanying drawings. Any means that can be devised to produce a better picture merits consideration. Most illustrators make extensive use of photography, pantographs and many other mechanical aids. There is no substitute for excellence of draftsmanship, to be sure, but this does not preclude the use of any means that will help produce a better picture.

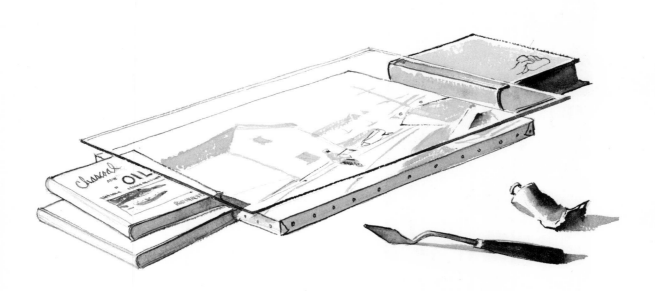

Copying

There is no field of human endeavor more democratic than the fraternity of artists. Art is an international, interracial language; "Idioma Universale," Goya called it. Or, as Constable put it, "In the eyes of the Almighty we are all duffers." The status of "student" is never really left by the artist. Titian regarded himself as only at the beginning of things when the plague carried him off at 99. Learning more of one's craft, of the secrets of nature, and of the old masters never ceases to be fascinating.

Copying has lost favor among some as a means of training and study. Many great artists of the past owe much of their training to this practice, however, and I feel that much can be gained from it in knowledge, taste, and enjoyment. Only excellent work should be copied, and of course the best procedure is to copy from the original. Most large museums permit copying and even supply certain facilities for copyists. Copying can also be done in your own home or studio from books or prints. Prints of fine drawings supply a wealth of knowledge. Color reproductions are somewhat less faithful representations of originals, but much can be learned from copying them nevertheless. The difference between merely looking at a painting and making a copy of it, is the difference between a casual acquaintance and intimate friendship.

Copies may be literal facsimiles of the original or they may be more in the nature of interpretations. Van Gogh's copies of Delacroix, Rubens, and other masters are interesting examples of the latter approach. He seems to have used the originals as foundations on which to experiment with his own restless and emotional style.

Interpretive copies of masterpieces can be done by the use of different media. For example, simple line drawings made with the object of exploring the lineal rhythms and movements of great paintings are most instruc-

This copy of a drawing by Rubens was made from a reproduction. Copying was once considered the accepted method of training the art student, and although it has lost favor somewhat in recent years, I believe it is still the best method of studying drawings and paintings. The act of copying reveals qualities not otherwise observed and gives the copyist a better understanding of the Master than any other form of study, in my opinion.

tive. Simplified tonal renderings in charcoal or watercolor are also useful in analyzing the abstract patterns in the design of great paintings. The design or compositional element of some paintings is not always conspicuously evident, but reveals itself through simplified lineal or tonal renderings.

A philosophy once prevailed among many artists that "great art was to conceal art." The force and dynamism of Grand Design was hidden and moved beneath the surface. In some contemporary painting an almost diametrically opposed idea seems to operate. An attempt is made to let the design element, or perhaps the color element, come forward and stand alone.

Other Media

While this book is fundamentally concerned with oil painting, other media have been mentioned from time to time. It is my firm conviction that the practice of painting in other media is beneficial to an understanding of the media in which you are most interested. Painting in watercolor or pastel is good for the oil painter and the reverse is also true. Staleness and an overconscious technique can be avoided by an open-minded use of various media. Graphic techniques, such as etching and lithography, should be explored too.

Priming Your Own Canvas

Many good, commercially prepared canvases are available in art supply stores. Some, however, are *not* so good and many artists find it expedient to prime their own. There are several very good reasons for doing so:
(1) Savings of 60 to 70 percent.
(2) Knowing exactly what ingredients are used.
(3) It is a simple procedure.
Here is my recommendation: Procure a good quality raw linen with an even, close, weave; the warp and woof being of the same weight thread. Tack or staple the linen to a stretcher frame. It should be flat and even but not tightly stretched, as some shrinkage will

be apparent in the next step, particularly in larger sizes.

Prepare a glue size by bringing one cup of water to a boil, *turn down heat,* and stir in four level tablespoons of ground rabbit skin glue. Add one more cup of hot water to mixture. (Avoid overheating the glue as it destroys its adhesive property.)

Brush this glue size onto the canvas. After a few hours sand lightly and apply a second coat. The purpose of sizing is to prevent the oils from impregnating the linen, which would cause the fabric to rot.

When the sizing has dried, apply white lead pigment as a priming. Use "Dutch Boy" white lead thinned slightly with turpentine to a semiliquid, or thin paste, consistency. Work the white lead into the grain of the canvas with a spatula or palette knife. Smooth it down with the knife and scrape off the excess. A second priming can be applied the next day. The canvas will be thoroughly dry and ready to use in about a week. It is well to make a project of priming several canvases at one time.

If a toned canvas is desired, add color to the priming. Other white pigments may be used, such as Zinc or Titanium, but white lead pro-

vides the toughest, most flexible film, and—most important of all—it is one of the *leanest* of all pigments. "Leaness" means that it contains less oil. The fundamental rule of painting, to ensure durability and prevent cracking (and this applies to house painting as well), is "Fat over lean." That is; the leaner coats should always be *under* the fatter. If a lean coat is applied over a fat (more oil content), cracking is almost certain to occur.

The reason white lead is not used more frequently in commercially primed canvas is that it tends to yellow slightly in rolls on the art supply dealers shelves, thus affecting its saleability. This does *not* seriously influence its permanence however. White lead is the white of the old masters and has been a major cornerstone of oil painting for at least five hundred years.

Grinding Your Own Colors

The grinding of colors by hand is also a simple procedure—at least in its fundamental aspects — and every artist should have some experience in it to acquaint himself with the nature of the materials he uses.

The pigment, which comes in a dry powder form, is first mixed on a sheet of glass or marble slab with enough linseed oil to make a heavy paste the consistency of peanut butter. The mixing is done with a large palette knife or spatula. Certain pigments will absorb more oil than others (the oil absorbency of some pigments is indicated in Appendix A). The amount of oil should be kept to a minimum.

The paste is then ground thoroughly on the slab with a glass muller. The paste must be frequently scraped together, and off the muller, with the palette knife. The grinding should continue until a smooth textured paint is achieved. Enough paint for a day's work can be made in a short while in this manner.

All pigments do not respond to grinding in the same way. Ultramarine blue, Veridian, and certain other pigments offer more resistance to being made into a smooth buttery consistency. A small amount (up to 15 percent) of poppy oil added to the linseed oil helps to achieve the desired consistency. Too much

poppy oil weakens the paint film and slows the drying. Beeswax, Aluminum Stearate and other substances are sometimes added as stabilizers or plasticizers. Such additives are generally more concerned with the storage and marketability of the paints than with their use. The experienced artist may find interesting possibilities for experiments in this area, however, that may bear an intimate relationship to his particular approach or style.

The sketch above was made on the spot, in oil on canvas, 8 x 10 inches in size. The larger (20 x 24) canvas was painted later in the studio.

The black and white drawing below was a preliminary study (18 x 24) done in preparation for the oil (of the same size) reproduced in color as the frontispiece of this book.

The oil sketch above provided a preliminary for the painting on the page opposite. It was done on a 9 x 12 canvas at
Hug Point, on the Oregon coast, with a
late afternoon sun warming the sandstone
cliff. The larger painting (20 x 24) was
done on a smooth masonite panel, some
months and 3,000 miles removed from the
original. Both paintings were done alla
prima on a white ground.

Hug Point

Hudson Valley Art Association Prize, 1951

THE LIFE OF A PAINTING

Framing

A painting is not really finished until it is framed. The uniform enclosure of the frame is a necessary part of the composition. Some artists paint the picture, at least partially, in a frame in order to visualize its completing influence.

Most painters keep a few "standard" size frames in their studios in which to try paintings (see Appendix A). This inevitably leads to a somewhat limiting standardization of shapes and sizes, against which many contemporary painters feel inclined to rebel. At least one frame manufacturer has patented a frame that can be expanded and contracted to help the artists overcome this limitation. This frame is made of component parts that link together like beads on a string. I have not tried this frame, but it appears to supply a very real need as studio equipment.

Gilt, or otherwise highly finished frames, are expensive and most artists do not attempt to maintain a large stock of them.

The hazards to frames — through the handling of many pictures — in large group exhibitions makes the use of sturdy, simple frames almost imperative for such exhibitions. Many artists make their own frames or buy simple wood frames which they finish themselves. Some attractive effects can be achieved by the use of stains and pigments rubbed into the wood. Paste wax makes a good final coating.

Exhibitions

Most art magazines have a listing of large exhibitions to which artists are invited to submit work. Usually, these exhibitions are juried and the risk of disappointment in sending work to them must be recognized. Many communities have local exhibitions that are either not juried at all or, at any rate, are intended to encourage the amateur. These afford a worthwhile opportunity to show paintings, and works by "unknowns" sometimes arrive in important collections through such channels.

Care of Paintings

The usual way to protect paintings from surface dirt and harmful gases is to varnish them. One of the chief requirements for a picture varnish is that it be fairly easy to remove. The simple solution, natural resin varnishes, mastic or damar, have been standard for many years. At present, several synthetic resin varnishes are on the market, and many leading museums and artists have accepted their use. One of their principle virtues is that they can be removed by mild solvents, such as turpentine or mineral spirit, that will have little or no effect upon the paint. The cooked oil varnishes, such as copal or the kind used on furniture, should never be used on paintings, principally because they can not be removed without almost certain damage to the paint films.

All varnishes deteriorate or change color with time, usually much more rapidly than the paintings. Mastic, and to a lesser degree damar, have a tendency to "bloom" (a disturbing, bluish cloudiness). Yellowing and darkening are characteristics of all varnishes, some turning a dark brown. Mastic has the best gloss retention of all the picture varnishes, but contemporary taste does not seem to require the high gloss so highly prized in Victorian times.

A light retouch varnish may be sprayed on a painting within a few days. A full strength varnish should not be applied for at least six months. A dry day is best. If cold, gently warm both canvas and varnish. Use a soft, wide brush. Keep dust free until the varnish sets (less than an hour for the synthetic resins).

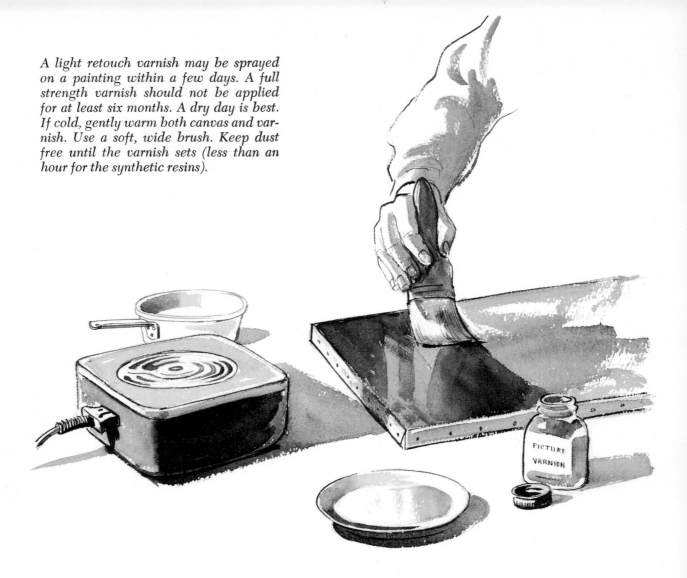

Before the advent of synthetic resins, the whole problem of varnishing paintings so troubled artists that some advanced the idea that it was better to use none at all. The practice of covering oil paintings with glass — in lieu of varnish — like watercolors, also gained some advocates. This is generally not satisfactory however, as the glass, which enhances a watercolor, imparts an annoying mirror-like effect to some oil paintings, and limits the viewing of the paint quality.

In storing paintings, it's best to keep them flat. If rolling is imperative, roll the canvas — paint side out—around a large cardboard tube. Avoid dampness, as water is the ancient enemy of paintings. Excess heat is also harmful.

In the schematic drawing opposite of a section through a painting: A, represents the varnish; B, the painting; C, the priming coat; D, the glue size; and E, the weave of the linen.

Craftsmanship

Modern science has contributed much toward the uniform working qualities of paints, to a knowledge of the fastness to light, and other characteristics of permanence in pigments and mediums. Manufacturers vie with each other to produce materials of ever increasing reliability and excellence. The artist need give little thought to anything but esthetic considerations. This "push-button" thinking, that gives us so much ease, is unfortunately not without its deleterious effects on the art of painting. The artist, in the process, has become so far separated from the basic fundamentals of his craft, involving an intimate familiarity with his materials, that valuable experience has been denied him. Some artists today have such little knowledge, and care so little about the nature of the very materials they use, that, in the eyes of Renaissance painters, they would be regarded as ignorant interlopers in their own studios.

Restoration

The subject of restoration is mentioned briefly because its study casts some light on the nature of the processes of painting. Restoration, or perhaps the term should more properly be "conservation," is in reality the care of paintings. It is the sense of responsibility we hope may be accorded our own paintings, applied to the paintings of our predecessors.

The anatomy of a painting consists of: the support, glue size, the ground, the paint film, and the varnish. The support in most paintings is a canvas, stretched on a wooden frame or stretcher. It may be some other continuous surface such as a wood panel, or a wall (in the case of a mural), but generally it is canvas. Canvas provides a strong, light surface on which to paint. Also, it permits easy access for purposes of restoration.

As the painting ages, the canvas often weakens first. It becomes brittle, and fragile, and the slightest blow may cause a break in the painting. The restorer corrects this condition by securing a new linen to the back of the old, to prevent further damage and wear. This is called relining. In rare cases the old canvas, or panel, is removed and replaced by a new one. This is called "transferring." This is a delicate and difficult operation and is only done if a flat, level condition cannot be achieved by relining. In the 18th and 19th Centuries some paintings moved from the Mediterranean to Northern Europe were transferred because of the excessive warping of the wood panels on which they were painted — due to the change of climate. In some cases paintings originally painted on panels were remounted on canvas. This is no longer considered sound practice, however, because of the difference in optical characteristics between the smooth wood panel and canvas, which was, inevitably imparted to the painting itself.

In the process of applying a new linen, a strong, penetrating adhesive is used, the object being to have it penetrate right to the back of the paint film, in order to securely anchor it in place. Pressure is sometimes applied, by

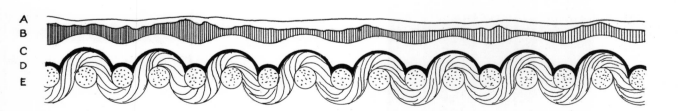

115

means of clamps or weights, and gentle heat is often applied, by ironing, to ensure penetration of the adhesive. The adhesive may be of the aqueous type, (rabbit skin glue, casein, etc.) or it may be a nonaqueous wax-resin combination, depending on the requirements of the situation confronting the restorer. Each type of adhesive has certain capabilities and limitations. The restorer, obviously, must be a man of experience and sound judgment.

In cleaning paintings, great knowledge and experience is also necessary. Much damage has been done by error and incompetence on the part of so-called restorers. A novice should never do more than a gentle dusting or vacuuming job on a painting. No liquid or semi-liquid should be applied to a painting except by an expert restorer. Water and even the mildest volatile solvents can be very harmful. A great temptation to overclean has led to irreparable damage and loss to some of the finest masterpieces. Even some of the world's great museums have been justly criticized on this score.

If paint or bits of canvas are missing, the area is filled with gesso, or picture putty, and "in-painted" to match the surrounding area. These patches are not apparent at a little distance, but can be easily found on close examination. The restorer's job is to restore the general appearance of the painting, not to commit forgery. Paintings, by artists well versed in their craft, are extraordinarily durable and with reasonable care should not require in-painting or other extreme measures to remain unchanged through many decades.

Seventeenth century painting by an unknown master, from the collection of the author, shown in the process of being cleaned. The canvas is marked off in squares with chalk and is painstakingly cleaned, one square at a time, with balls of cotton and the appropriate cleaning agent. The latter must be carefully formulated for each painting to be cleaned by making tests at the extreme edge of the canvas.

EQUIPMENT AND MATERIALS

Paint Box

There are many types of artist's paint box manufactured. Choose from among them one that is of suitable size to carry everything you need, but not so large it is unwieldy. The 12 x 16 inch size is most popular. Wood is the traditional material for paint boxes, but the newer all-metal types offer practical advantages. They are not subject to splitting, and the hinges and other fittings are more securely fastened to the box. Be sure the fittings for closing the box are well made. The spectacle of a paint box popping open, to spill its contents all over the place, is enough to give one the Irrawaddy chills.

Palette

Most paint boxes come equipped with a square wood palette that fits in the box in such a way that wet paint can be left on it without too much hazard. The habit of trying to save little dabs of paint is a bad one, however. It is much better to wipe the palette clean after each use, and start with fresh color.

It would take a busy painter a life time to save enough in left-over paint, to buy, say, one filling for the gas tank of his car. The evil habit of skimping on paint, on the other hand, can still forever the well-springs of abundance that must be poured into any work of art.

Palettes made of many sheets of paper, bound together with a stiff cardboard backing, are convenient. They are cleaned by simply tearing off the top sheet. They come in several sizes.

The oval wood palette of tradition seems to be going the way of the dodo. They are not too practical, but are truly beautiful, and I, for one, feel inclined to shed a bitter tear at their passing.

Palette Cups

These are, fortunately, inexpensive and should be purchased a dozen at a time. In the studio you are forever in need of an extra one for some new "brew" you wish to try. Two inch size cups are best for studio use. For outdoor sketching, the 1½ inch size is adequate.

Some palette cups are joined together in pairs—like Siamese twins—why, I will never know. I prefer the single variety. Another complaint I have about palette cups is that the clip arrangement on the bottom seldom has enough spring to hold it securely on the palette, and I hope some enterprising manufacturer reads this and is moved to remedy the shortcoming.

Palette Knives

The need for a variety of palette knives will only be felt as one gains in experience. This is true — and rightly so — of much of the equipment of the artist. Any technical step that is taken in response to a deeply felt need, usually turns out to be a real stride along the path of achievement.

The rather long spatula is best for mixing paint on the palette. Some of the smaller, more flexible, knives are used in painting. I have one large, very sturdy knife with a sharp edge, that is great for scraping things.

Easels

A good sketching easel can fill all needs — except for very large canvases. I have one made of aluminum that is very versatile. It has rubber "feet" so it will not mar or slip on a polished floor. Its legs can telescope so that it can be used on a table. Metal fittings are interchangeable with the rubber tips for rough terrain. It has a practical device at the top for holding a canvas at any angle. When set up, it forms a platform on which to rest the palette.

For many years I used a wooden, English made, sketching easel of which I was very fond. I am conservative by nature, and I only grudgingly yielded to the charms of the aluminum paragon of the machine age; but my conversion has been complete and without qualification. As far as I am concerned, the aluminum easel is here to stay — it is tops!

A good studio easel is something else again. It is a piece of furniture. Something to live with. It stands solidly — like Fort Knox — or moves ponderously on large swivelled castors. It can make you feel insignificant in its august presence, or it can buck you up to greater things. It is a delicious luxury. I have two.

The Maul Stick

To "maul" is to "paint" in German — hence a maul stick is a painting stick. It is used as a hand rest for the application of small strokes involved in rendering details. For studio use a maul stick about a yard long is best, especially for larger canvases. A blackboard pointer makes a good substitute, but the standard type, wood or aluminum maul stick is better. They are usually jointed, so they can be shortened for smaller paintings, or for carrying in the paint box, and are equipped with a cork ball on the end for resting against the canvas if necessary.

Brushes

The best formula I can suggest regarding brushes, is to buy the top grade offered by well-known, reliable, art suppliers. They are expensive, but you don't need many, and they last a long time.

There are two main classifications in oil painting brushes: bristle and sable. These are made in long hair, known as "flats" and short hair called "brights." There are also "rounds." They range in size from one-eighth inch in width, to two inches, and are usually designated by number.

The difference in characteristics between the sable, and bristle brushes, is very marked. The bristle has much more "spring" and vigor, and longer wear than the sable. Its stroke is in harmony with the surface of canvas, and it is most favored in the bold, textural, approach of much contemporary painting.

The sable is softer, more subtle in stroke, and wears down rather quickly when used on a rough surface. It is most useful for blending, and expressing smooth texture.

The difference between flats, brights, and rounds — in either sable or bristle — is less definitive. In the final analysis, the use of brushes (and this applies to other equipment also) becomes intimately associated with an individual's "style." Style, in this sense, being an equation of personal preferences, experience, knowledge, and background.

My recommendation is that a beginner use as few brushes as possible at first (about four) and add one at a time as a need is felt, or a desire is experienced, to cross a frontier from a familiar to a less known realm.

There are other brushes to try in addition to the more standard types. One, called a "filbert," resembles a slightly worn bright. (Incidentally, any brush changes its character as it wears — often for the better.) Another, most impressive looking brush, is the "badger blender." My personal opinion is that its looks far outweigh its usefulness.

Small house painters' brushes are useful for artistic painting. One called a "sash tool" was the principal painting brush of the landscape painter, Chauncey Ryder. A two-inch varnish brush is also necessary.

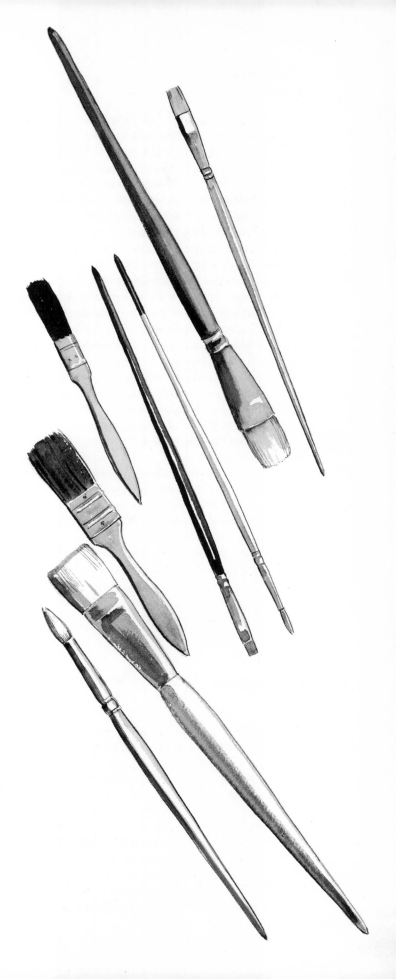

Supports

The traditionally favored support on which to paint is linen canvas, stretched on a wooden frame. It is strong, light, and durable.

Cotton is less desirable than linen. Linen-cotton mixtures are less desirable still, because of their lack of uniformity of absorption and variation of tensions. Jute offers interesting surfaces, but becomes very brittle on short aging and should not be used for permanent painting.

Patented wooden stretcher strips with interlocking corners come in inch-divisible sizes up to about 50 inches and are easily fitted together. Larger sized stretcher frames, or the type with cross supports mortised in, must be ordered specially.

The conscientious artist will always sandpaper or plane the edge of a stretcher to prevent breaking of the canvas threads where they pass over the wood. Canvas is stretched with a tool called stretcher pliers, and tacked or stapled in place.

Canvas covered cardboards in various sizes are widely distributed for student use. They are convenient and inexpensive, but are not recommended for permanent painting.

Panels, such as wood or masonite, are appropriate supports for painting, particularly if a smooth surface is desired. The two great hazards to the wood panels of the Renaissance — wood worms and warping — are eliminated in the hard, durable, masonite.

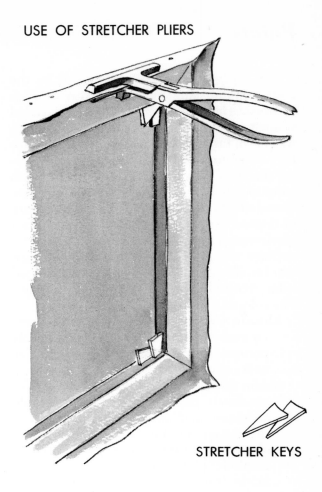

USE OF STRETCHER PLIERS

STRETCHER KEYS

Grounds

Canvas or panels are prepared for painting by application of a glue size and one or more coats of "priming" or "ground." White oil paint or gesso is the usual ground. Sometimes colored pigment, red or gray, etcetera is added to the ground. The ground is worked into the sized canvas by means of a spatula. Several coats of ground will hide some of the texture of even a coarse canvas. If desired, a texture can be imparted to the ground by stippling the last coat. This is done with a large, stiff brush called a "stippling" brush.

Some Standard Frame Sizes

Frames can be made in any size, of course, but most art supply stores and frame shops carry ready made frames in popular sizes, as follows:

8″ x 10″	20″ x 24″
9″ x 12″	22″ x 28″
10″ x 14″	24″ x 30″
12″ x 16″	25″ x 30″
14″ x 18″	30″ x 36″
16″ x 20″	30″ x 40″

Paints

The top grades of colors supplied by the most reputable manufacturers are recommended as in the case of brushes. The so-called student grades are cheaper, but are apt to be weaker in tinting power, less stable, and since they don't go as far, the saving is more apparent than real. More important still, learning to paint is largely a matter of developing habits, so one should become familiar with, and learn to depend on, materials that will serve your whole career.

Color manufacturers will supply information on all their colors, or it can be obtained from artists' handbooks (see bibliography). The colors I use are described below:

Alizarin Crimson: Made from anthracene (a coal tar derivative). It is reasonably permanent, very high in oil absorbtion, and a slow drier.

Indian Red: Pure iron oxide. Very opaque, absolutely permanent, medium in oil absorbancy, and an average drier. It produces a strong film.

Cadmium Red Light: Three parts cadmium sulphide plus two parts cadmium selenide. It is very opaque, very permanent, and a very slow drier. It produces a fairly strong film and is medium in oil absorbancy rate.

Cadmium Orange: Cadmium sulphide; its characteristics are similar to Cadmium Red Light.

Cadmium Yellow: Same as Cadmium Orange.

Cadmium Yellow Light: Same as Cadmium Orange.

Yellow Ochre: A native clay, opaque, and absolutely permanent. It is a slow drier, is medium in oil absorbancy, and produces a fairly strong film.

Raw Umber: A native earth, it is not entirely opaque. Absolutely permanent. It is a fast drier and produces a tough, flexible film. It has high oil absorbancy.

Burnt Sienna: A native earth that has been roasted. It is permanent. It is a rapid drier, and produces a hard, fairly strong film. It is high in oil absorbancy.

Viridian: Hydrated chromium hydroxide. It is transparent and very permanent. Very high in oil absorbancy, it has a medium drying rate. Produces a hard flexible film.

Cobalt Blue: Compound of cobalt oxide, aluminum oxide, and phosphoric acid. It is very permanent and nearly transparent. It has a very high oil absorbancy rate, is an average drier, and produces a rather brittle film.

Ultramarine Blue: Colloidal sulphur; it is permanent and semi-transparent. It has a medium oil absorbancy rating and is a slow drier. It produces a fairly hard, somewhat brittle film.

Ivory Black: Charred ivory (or bone). It is permanent, high in oil absorbancy rate and a very slow drier; it produces a rather soft film.

Flake White: Basic lead carbonate. It is permanent, except that exposed films will turn yellow or brownish if acted upon by air polluted with sulphur fumes. This is a negligible defect, since it can be protected by varnish. (It is the white of the old masters). It dries rapidly to a tough, flexible film, and has a low oil absorbancy index.

The above constitutes my basic palette. I sometimes supplement it with one of the other permanent colors, or whites, if necessary. It is well to avoid any of the colors of doubtful permanence lest one become attached to them and establish a habit that may be hard to lose.

Mediums

The mediums I regularly use are as follows:

Turpentine: The kind sold in hardware, or paint stores, labelled "Pure Gum Spirit" is pleasant smelling and satisfactory for all uses.

Linseed Oil: Refined linseed oil of a pale golden or light amber color is the best as it has less tendency to "yellow" than some of the lighter varieties which tend to revert to a deeper tone on aging.

Stand Oil: A polymerized linseed oil of about the consistency of honey, especially useful in glazes or where its tendency to "level" is desired.

Rectified Petroleum: A refined mineral spirit, used as a solvent for synthetic resins, etc.

Damar: A natural resin gathered from forests in the East Indies. It is soluble in turpentine. Six and a quarter (6¼) ounces of damar resin dissolved in ten fluid ounces of turpentine makes a concentration known as five pound cut (5 lbs. per gallon of turpentine). This makes an average concentration. It can be used as an ingredient in glaze mediums in this strength. Thinned slightly with turpentine it serves as a final picture varnish. Thinned about 3 to 1 with turpentine it forms a basic retouch varnish. The addition of a very little anhydrous alcohol and a small amount of stand oil improves this retouch varnish.

Synthetic Resins: These are usually of the acrylic or vinyl type and are mixed with mineral spirit. These may be used as final varnish or as retouch varnish. They are usually in about the same proportion — resin to solvent — as the damar.

Glaze Medium: One part stand oil, one part damar varnish and 3 to 5 parts turpentine makes a basic glaze medium.

Variations of the above ingredients will provide variations in the character of the glaze medium. Recipes for glaze mediums using many other ingredients are also possible.

The subject of mediums, both for glazing and other manipulations of paint, has long been a source of fascination to artists. Interesting theories have been expounded, concerning studio secrets possessed by certain painters, or schools of painting, that have been lost and are therefore subject to rediscovery — like pirate treasure. Recipes from old manuscripts are constantly being tried.

To compound the confusion in such matters, the nomenclature of materials — confusing enough at best — has changed, over the years. This is partly brought about by the fact that most artists' materials are no longer solely the products of the studios, but are rather minor by-products, of the large paint and varnish industry. The term "copal" for instance, once was fairly specific, and referred to Kauri, an expensive, highly esteemed, fossil resin from New Zealand. It now can be legitimately applied to many resins having widely varied properties and generally refers to a cooked varnish containing a high percentage of rosin and driers. It should not, in any case, be used for permanent painting.

The foregoing covers the major materials of oil painting. There are many other items that have minor uses in the studio and the list is as varied as the number of artists, and is constantly changing. The student is earnestly enjoined to retain an open mind and be on the alert for all possibilities to further his knowledge and experience. Artistic expression is irrevocably wedded to technical matters — in fact it's an important part of the fun. Good Painting!

GLOSSARY OF OIL PAINTING TERMS

Aerial Perspective: The difference in the appearance of any given color brought about by its nearness or distance from the eye. It is usually thought of as the coolness or "blueness" imparted by considerable distance such as far away hills.

Alla Prima: Direct, one-coat painting. The technique of achieving the desired effect with as few brush strokes or manipulations as possible.

Bloom: A foggy effect that appears on some varnished surfaces, said to be caused by a form of mold.

Bole: A red earth (similar to Venetian or Indian Red) used to color the ground in certain olders schools of painting and revived by some moderns.

Chiaroscuro: Light and shade. The term is usually used to describe strong light and shadow effects.

Contour: The undulations of the surface of any form as expressed in drawing or painting.

Cool: See Thermal.

Embu: A dull spot in an otherwise glossy surface.

Eye Level: The level plane in which your eyes are located. It becomes the horizon at the limit of vision, or is a line drawn at eye level for the purpose of establishing perspective.

Fat Over Lean: The principal that a continuous paint layer should not be superimposed over another unless the underlying layer is "leaner" (having less oil content) than the upper layer. This applies to the ground or priming on the canvas as well as to layers in the painting itself. Extensive contravention of this principal will cause cracking or other defects in a painting.

Filler: Inert pigment.

Fixative: A thin, quick-drying varnish which is applied, by spraying, to charcoal or pastel drawings to prevent smudging.

Fugitive: As applied to color it means not permanent. Subject to fading.

Gesso: A paint, or plastic paste, made with an aqueous binder (either glue, casein, or gelatin) and whiting, chalk, or slaked plaster of paris. It is used as a painting ground or for modeling and repairing (as in frames).

Glaze: A thin application of color applied over dried color or toned underpainting. A glaze is generally darker than the underpainting.

Grisaille: A technique of monochrome painting in gray, usually as an underpainting in preparation for glazing with colors.

Ground: An even coating applied to the support on which to paint, also called "priming." It may be an aqueous — gesso type material, or oil paint. It may be white or colored.

Hiding Power: Degree of opacity in paint, its ability to cover.

Impasto: Thick, heavy paint.

Imprimatura: A thin preliminary tone applied over the ground.

Inert Pigment: A powdered substance mixed with colored pigments, imparting no appreciable change. They are sometimes used as adulterants or cheapeners, but may also be used to improve working qualities.

In-painting: Filling in, with matching colors, those areas missing from damaged paintings.

Local Color: The actual color of something, as opposed to the apparent color. A local color is modified in appearance by its surrounding colors and by distance.

Marouflage: Securing a canvas to a wall by an adhesive — as a mural.

Maul Stick: Painting stick, used to steady the hand in painting.

Media: The mode of artistic expression or the actual instrument, or material, used. (Also expressed as medium).

Medium: The liquid constituent of a paint, particularly that added in painting as opposed to that added in manufacture (see vehicle).

Middle Value: The broad lights (not counting high lights) and broad shadows (not including those small, darker touches called accents). The middle values cover most of the area, carry most of the illusion. The high lights and accents are the finishing touches.

Mixed Technique: A method of painting employing both aqueous (tempera) colors and oil colors in alternate layers.

Palette: Surface used for mixing paint, also the particular assortment of colors used by an artist.

Picture Putty: A putty made of whiting and stand oil, used in leveling up broken places in damaged paintings. Gesso is also used for this, but is very brittle and may crack if the area is extensive.

Pigments: Dry, powdered materials used in making paints to provide the color. Also "inert" pigments used in paint manufacture which do not impart color but are stabilizers, plasticizers or adulterants.

Retouch Varnish: A light, quick-drying varnish sprayed or painted in a thin coat over a partly finished painting. Its function is to make all parts of the painting appear equally wet and fresh. It also serves to isolate the underlying paint from superimposed touches.

Scumbling: A thin application of color similar to a glaze, except that, while a glaze is darker than the underpainting, scumbling is lighter.

Thermal: In reference to color this term means the degree of warmth or coolness (also called the "temperature"). The warmth refers to the warm appearing colors: red, yellow, brown. The cool colors are those that tend toward blue. The terms are often used *relatively*. For example, one may refer to a "cool" red or a "warm" blue.

Underpainting: The underlying body of a painting. The term usually refers to a planned method rather than successive layers built up in a trial and error process to arrive at an effect.

Values (tone values): The degree of darkness or light in any given area of a subject or picture. Sometimes expressed "color values" when referring to a painting rather than a drawing. The term means the same, however, as every color is also a value.

Vanishing Point: A point, in perspective at which lines parallel to each other will converge if extended.

Vehicle: The liquid ingredient in paint, usually that involved in its manufacture rather than added in painting (see medium).

Veil: A thin glaze of color, usually applied over an entire painting or ground.

Verdaccio: A greenish underpainting observable in many old masters.

Warm: See Thermal.

BIBLIOGRAPHY

A Manual of Design, by Janet K. Smith, Reinhold, New York, 1950

An Atlas of Anatomy for Artists, by Fritz Schider. Dover, New York, 1947

An Atlas of Animal Anatomy for Artists, by Ellenberger, Baum, and Dittrich. Dover, New York, 1949

Analysis of Beauty, by William Hogarth, edited by Joseph Burke. Oxford University Press, New York, 1955

Artists' Pigments, by Frederick W. Weber. Van Norstrand, New York, 1923

Atlas of Human Anatomy, by Stephen Rogers Peck. Oxford University Press, New York, 1951

Creative Perspective, by Ernest W. Watson. Reinhold, New York, 1955

Paint, Paintings, and Restoration, by Maximilian Toch. Van Norstrand, New York, 1931

Perspective, by Frank Medworth. Scribners, New York, 1937

Perspective Made Easy, by Ernest R. Norling. Macmillan, New York, 1939

Practical Application of Dynamic Symmetry, by Jay Hambidge. Yale University Press, 1932

The Artist's Handbook, by Ralph Mayer. Viking, New York, 1940

The Materials of the Artist, by Max Doerner. Harcourt Brace, New York, 1934

The Secret Formula and Techniques of the Masters, by Jacques Maroger. Studio Publications, New York, 1948

INDEX OF ARTISTS AND SUBJECTS

Note: Consult the Table of Contents for main subjects treated at length in the text. Also see Appendix A for a detailed discussion of EQUIPMENT AND MATERIALS, *Appendix B for a* GLOSSARY OF OIL PAINTING TERMS.

(Continued from previous page)